Cordelia Strube won the CBC Literary Competition in 1987 for her radio play Mortal; and in the following four years wrote 10 plays for radio. To date, she has published nine funny, powerful and critically-acclaimed novels, among them *Alex & Zee, Teaching Pigs to Sing, The Barking Dog, Lemon and Miłosz.*

Winner of the Toronto Arts Foundation Protégé Award, she has been long-listed for the Scotia Giller, short-listed for the Governor General's Award, the Prix Italia, the Books In Canada First Novel, The Re-Lit, and the Trillium. Ms. Strube has been leading writing workshops at Ryerson University since 2000.

Barry Healey has written television variety material for such performers as Milton Berle, Arte Johnson, Soupy Sales, Bob Crane, Andy Griffith, Jackie Mason, Henry Mancini, Van Johnson and others. His motion picture credits include the award-winning shorts: OUTTAKES (1977) writer / director/ producer; THE NIGHT BEFORE THE MORNING AFTER (1979) writer/director; and the feature films: THE GREY FOX (1983) co-producer; ONE MAGIC CHRISTMAS (1985) writer; BIG DEAL (1985) director; HOLLYWOOD NORTH (2003) writer. Mr. Healey's 1st novel, *The Sex Life of the Amoeba*, was published in the Fall of 2014.

EXHiLaRATinG PROSE

EXHiLaRATinG PROSE

COGNITIONS, CONTEMPLATIONS,
INSIGHTS, INTROSPECTIONS,
LUCUBRATIONS, MEDITATIONS,
MUSINGS, PROGNOSTICATIONS,
REFLECTIONS, REVERIES & RUMINATIONS
ON THE PROCESS OF WRITING

by
Barry Healey & Cordelia Strube

Illustrations by Barry Healey

Baraka
Books

Montréal

ISBN 978-1-77186-038-3 pbk; 978-1-77186-041-3 epub; 978-1-77186-042-0 pdf; 978-1-77186-043-7 mobi/kindle

All illustrations including cover by Barry Healey
Cover by Folio infographie
Book design by Folio infographie
Legal Deposit, 2nd quarter 2015

Bibliothèque et Archives nationales du Québec
Library and Archives Canada

Published by Baraka Books of Montreal.
6977, rue Lacroix
Montréal, Québec H4E 2V4
Telephone: 514 808-8504
info@barakabooks.com
www.barakabooks.com

Printed and bound in Quebec

Baraka Books acknowledges the generous support of its publishing program from the Société de développement des entreprises culturelles du Québec (SODEC), the Government of Quebec, tax credit for book publishing administered by SODEC, and the Canada Council for the Arts.

We acknowledge the financial support of the Government of Canada, through the National Translation Program for Book Publishing for our translation activities and through the Canada Book Fund (CBF) for our publishing activities.

Trade Distribution & Returns
Canada and the United States
Independent Publishers Group
1-800-888-4741 (IPG1);
orders@ipgbook.com

To Carson

"A page of good prose remains invincible."

—John Cheever

"A certain ruthlessness and a sense of alienation from society is as essential to creative writing as it is to armed robbery. The strong-armer isn't out merely to turn a fast buck any more than the poet is out solely to see his name on the cover of a book... What both need most deeply is to get even."

—Nelson Algren, *The Paris Review*

"The greatest possible mint of style is to make the words absolutely disappear into the thought."

—Nathaniel Hawthorne

Contents

Where Does Good Prose Come From?

Musings.

And from where do the musings come?

Everywhere: scraps of conversation, rants, soliloquies, images, diatribes, letters, memos, grocery lists, horoscopes, sightings, phone calls, emails, and text messages—those written, oral, or visual parings that swarm our conscious and subconscious minds.

Most brain activity is concerned with function only (i.e. breathing, picking up the dry-cleaning), but a small part of the brain compulsively wants to make sense of our existence, and musings are the sparks that ignite those written and spoken explanations.

Some of these sparks we fashion into stories, which we tell in cafes, offices, streets, homes, bars, washrooms, clubs, barns, arenas, funeral homes, sports clubs, bingo halls, trains, airports; in books, movies, and on TV, over the internet and on our cells. Imagine, everywhere on Planet Earth, at this exact moment, hundreds of millions of us are telling tales.

"Stories... connect the visible with the invisible, the present with the past. They propose life as something of moral consequence. They distribute the suffering so that it can be borne... there was a time when there would have been nothing but stories, and no sharper distinction between what was fact and what was invented than between what was spoken and what was sung... Stories were the first repositories of human knowledge. They were as important to survival as the spear or hoe."

—E.L. Doctorow, *Creationists*

The beginnings of literature, as we know it, arrived around four thousand years ago, when a few lone *compelled ones*, having strung together lengthy poems, wandered through the countryside declaiming them to whomever would listen. These epic tales were not written down, but committed to memory (easier in verse), a prodigious feat if you consider their length—over fifteen thousand lines for Homer's *Iliad* and over twelve thousand for his *Odyssey*. Eventually, to ensure that the death of the storyteller did not bring about the death of the story, the poets and others began etching these stories onto papyrus, animal skins, and finally paper—the act of writing as we know it. In Western culture, for the past two millennia, the *compelled ones*—Homer, Aristotle, Seneca, Shakespeare, Pepys and Johnson et al—have assiduously contributed to the ongoing narrative of the Great Chain of Being, seeking life's meaning through the recording of stories of our frailties and exuberances. Their plays, epic poems, diaries, journals and, finally, novels have linked us to the joys and sufferings (mostly sufferings, it would seem) of our predecessors, the value of which is surprising—the dinosaurs left only old bones and fossil fuels behind.

"A human being is nothing but a story with skin around it."
—Fred Allen

"Writers don't have lifestyles. They sit in little rooms and write."
—Norman Mailer

Although trapped currently in the Age of the Screen, we still refer to the printed word; and the *compelled ones* persist—scribbling in lonely rooms, assembling and reassembling their musings into various forms of prose. Consumed by doubt, some will risk exposing their manuscripts to workshop gatherings, hoping to tighten their narratives, and begin to find an audience.

Good prose is the result of countless rewrites. The time required to make prose live on the page is daunting, for the sentences and paragraphs will not startle or fascinate unless distilled to a fine essence. The *compelled ones* write unceasingly all their lives. J.D. Salinger didn't retire—he stopped publishing in his mid-forties—but continued to create stories almost until his death at age ninety-five.

"Prose is like hair; it shines with combing."

—Gustave Flaubert

Many of the following oddities, notions, and conjectures have been generated over the years by the shared experiences of sitting alone in rooms, staring at computer screens, and from the feedback of writing workshops. Assembling these thoughts into one document, we hope to reinvigorate the reader's imagination. As Johann Wolfgang von Goethe once observed, "Everything has been thought of before, but the problem is to think of it again."

"We're going to spend all summer looking at this thing. On one piece of drawing paper or one canvas and we're going to look at it exactly the way it is. Then we're going to keep working on it until we kill it. And then we're going to keep working on it until it comes back on its own."

—Willem de Kooning

First, let's examine '*The Speaks*'.

"Literature is, primarily, a chain of connections from the past to the present. It is not reinvented every morning, as some bad writers like to believe."

—Gore Vidal

1. Dead Language – The Speaks

What is it?

Dead language is language that is... dead. Like the Monty Python parrot, it is deceased, expired, no longer of the living. It litters the cultural landscape. It's un-arousing, leaden, repetitive, and comprised of stagnant words and phrases unable to stimulate the reader.

You cannot create living—breathing—prose with dead language. To snare the reader's attention, you need to replace mirthless, incoherent, and disingenuous words with startling and lucid ones. Sparse, supple, and vivid writing stimulates the reader's imagination. Each word and phrase, each sentence, must be honed to its precise meaning before being deployed—effective prose is uncluttered, containing no tired, needless, bland, or deceptive language which could smother imagery or meaning.

> "A writer is somebody for whom writing is more difficult than it is for other people."
> —Thomas Mann

Conversely, dead language—'The Speaks': ad-speak, media-speak, techno-speak, medical-speak, valley-girl-speak, art-speak, hip-speak, sports-speak, corporate-speak, government-speak, and hundreds of other speaks—contains clusters of clichéd words and phrases, which endlessly replicate common oral and written syntax, effectively nuking the communication of forceful and original ideas.

Ad-speak—like "Doublethink" in Orwell's *1984*—is now wholly meaningless (e.g. our local jazz radio station advertises "This commercial-free Sunday is brought to you by..."). Everywhere in the media we are bombarded with meaningless jargon—it's easy to imagine chimps bouncing on chairs in ad agency cubicles, pounding on keyboards and chanting, "the more you save, the more you buy, the more you buy, the more you save."

> "Advertising is the rattling of a stick inside a swill bucket."
>
> —George Orwell

Ad agencies insist they practice the 'Art of Persuasion'; but wouldn't the 'Art of Deception' be more accurate? Ad-speak practitioners rely particularly on dead language, using repetitive, clichéd superlatives to describe the merchandise or services they hawk, especially when these items have no intrinsic, or exceptional, value (i.e. selling the "sizzle" and not the steak).

Most corporate advertising is built around vague, suggestive slogans, designed to mislead, and which, when questioned, appear fatuous:

"Making things happen" (like climate change, Toyota?)
"It's good to talk" (do you listen, British Telecom?)
"Things go better with Coke" (what things, Coke, obesity?)
"Fox News – Fair and balanced" (fair to whom, Rupert?)
"Doctors recommend Phillip Morris" (dead doctors?)
"You can be sure of Shell" (sure of what, Shell, oil spills?)
"An army of one"
(are you counting on *both* hands, Pentagon?)

"Think Different" (shouldn't you go first, Apple?)
"Rediscover delicious harmony"
(delicious or *nutritious*, McDonalds?)

Ad-speak is employed to seduce and reassure, using vague *non sequiturs* presented in rhythmic, inane phrases. Ikea seems to stand alone with its plain and witty, "Screw yourself."

Business-speak (a cousin to ad-speak?) is possibly the greatest purveyor of dead language in our culture (e.g. course descriptions in business school calendars). It utilizes abstract, overworked phrases such as "our tradition of excellence in..." and "forward-thinking attitudes of our staff," along with "to serve the public," to lull consumers into believing that they're receiving value for money, and to obscure questionable business practices. Would any company that manufactures a viable, useful, and lasting product use dead language to promote its goods or services—if those goods and services were highly regarded?

> "Writing is like prostitution. First you do it for the love of it, then you do it for a few friends, and finally you do it for the money."
>
> —Molière

"I grew up on a farm. I know what it means to restore the land," says Garrett, a youthful "environmental coordinator" for ConocoPhillips, standing in a forest in a (full-page) magazine ad. Garrett is being disingenuous. His phlegmatic statement is intended to imply that the damage caused by the oil industry's Canadian tar-sands operations—a forty-metre-deep gouge in northern Alberta's boreal forest the size of the state of Delaware, considered by ecologists and scientists the most environmentally destructive project on the planet—will be magically restored but doesn't indicate *how*.

Garrett's knowing "what it means to restore the land" is senseless ad-speak. Oil industry representatives have no idea how to regenerate the boreal forest (unless it knows something the Gaia doesn't); and to cloak their malfeasance, they refer to their decimation of the landscape as "oil sands." If these were truly "oil sands," it would be a simple matter to extract the oil from the sand. As it is, the oil is locked inside *tar* (or bitumen), and the industry consumes millions of cubic feet of natural gas to heat millions of gallons of *fresh* water to separate the oil from the tar; hence the appellation "tar sands." The spent water, permeated with toxic chemicals, is then pumped into large depressions called tailings ponds (the size of small lakes), from which it seeps into, and poisons, the watershed.

In the same oil-industry-financed campaign (another full-page ad), Megan, a young biologist employed by Devon Energy, squatting in a wetland, tells us that she is "monitoring the plants, soil, and animals." "We know," she says, "what was here before, what's here now, and what we need to do before we leave." What, Megan, what?

"The purpose of a writer is to keep civilization from destroying itself."
—Albert Camus

Each year, in the form of advertising, millions of dollars are expended on dead language by 'resource' (fossil fuel and mining) industries needing to mask their assault on the natural world. These corporations presume that by presenting Garrett and Megan's handsome, youthful, and educated presence, and their Pollyannaesque comments, they will quell public apprehension, but industry rhetoric—as murky and toxic as a tailings pond—along with rapacious business methods, are to be seen more as weapons of mass destruction.

"Water (the ads further inform us) is an important part of oil and gas production, and as Canada's oil and gas industry grows, so does demand on Canadian water resources." This sentence, cowering on the page, suggests that the oil industry is deeply concerned about the preservation of fresh water—but if so, why are they poisoning so much of it? And why aren't Garrett and Megan informing their lubricious bosses that poisoning millions of gallons of fresh water and decimating our boreal forests for profit are, ultimately, acts not only of greed but of imbecility?

These examples of corporate-speak suggest action where none exists, as in "our team will explore specific environmental goals." The word "explore"—like Megan's use of the word "monitor"—paired with the words "specific" and "goals" is intended to raise expectations that action is being taken; but what? The "monitoring" and "exploring" involve no commitment—nothing is being done to rectify, proscribe or initiate action. The 'team' only explores; the word "specific" is being used to suggest focus but, again, on what? "Our team will explore specific environmental goals," hopes to reassure us that the problem is being dealt with; but if it were, would such pusillanimous words and phrases need to be employed? With multibillions of dollars at stake—and having no idea of how to restore *their* "Hiroshima" (according to Neil Young)—these (government-subsidized) resource corporations attempt to neuter public opinion by retaining more consultants to conduct further "monitoring" and "exploring," yielding additional reports in dead language. In this way, these ongoing deceptions allow them to continue— unfettered—their destruction of our once pristine landscape.

Corporate-speak is similar to government-speak, both reliant on technology and dead language to nullify access. When was the last time you attempted to contact a large corporation or government agency, and were able to speak with a live human being to obtain the information or service you needed?

Dead language is also prevalent in the medical (doctor-speak), legal (lawyer-speak), and building (archi-speak) professions. Architects, when bidding on new projects, employ abstract phrases in their design proposals to convey an aura of proficiency, but what do the phrases "flexible activity rooms," "needs assessment analysis" and "presentation forums" actually mean? Aren't they 'puff' phrases meant to gull the client? Is a "flexible activity room" the boudoir of a dominatrix? And what would a "presentation forum" look like? How many humans—or Martians—might it hold? Is it likely to contain an "organic simplicity" (as Frank Lloyd Wright once hoped)?

And what should a "building of excellence" look like? Would it resemble a triangle, a stilted box, or—even stranger—an inexplicable eruption of jagged, irregular-shaped steel and glass pyramids jutting out randomly at all angles, capriciously affixed to a once-elegant, now sadly disfigured, historical edifice? Could there be a symbiotic relationship between the many misshapen structures that litter our urban landscape and architectural design proposals replete with dead prose?

"The problem with so much of today's literature is the clumsiness of its artifice—the conspicuous disparity between what writers are aiming for and what they actually achieve. Theirs is a remarkably crude form of affectation: a prose so repetitive, so elementary in its syntax, and so numbing in its overuse of wordplay that it often demands less concentration than the average "genre" novel. Even today's obscurity is easy, the sort of gibberish that stops all thought dead in its tracks."

—B.R. Myers,
A Reader's Manifesto

In literature, the rampant use of clichés (the sign of a dying language) is relentless: "hearts lurching," "hearts pounding" or "pounding hearts," "racing minds and hearts," "leaping / sinking / stopping hearts and lurching stomachs," "breaking into a smile," "pangs of (anything)," "seizing, or lumps in, throats or stomachs, sinking stomachs, and tightening throats" submerge the reader into a quagmire of inane jargon.

The words "smile" and "laugh" (as noun and verb) are written frequently. Why? With so many other words available to describe these basic human responses, their repetition seems indicative of a barren or lazy imagination. Do the perpetrators of clichés think that we will find comfort in familiar words and phrases rendered senseless by overuse? Or do they fear that new words and forceful expressions might intimidate or confuse the reader?

Dead language kills thought and stifles originality. To convey meaning, and to avoid smothering the willing reader in a miasma of turgid prose, stories need to be told with penetrating simplicity.

The canny writer should know that the reader is not dull-witted; yet here in the Canadian literary landscape, an organization exists that funds authors to write novels on the condition that they avoid using 'unfamiliar' words (e.g. "muted"), which might baffle the reader. This covert form of censorship, reminiscent of Orwell's "Newspeak" in *1984*, demonstrates ignorance of the reading process. With any well-written work, the reader

"Those whom books will hurt will not be proof against events. If some books are deemed more baneful and their sale forbid, how, then, with deadlier facts, not dreams of doting men? Events, not books, should be forbid."

—Herman Melville

will not necessarily comprehend every single word, but if the story and the writing are engaging, he or she will bypass words which they might be seeing for the first time and will come across again, eventually surmising their meaning from the context (see the John Holt anecdote in *The Stillness of Reading*, page 157).

Isn't this how an enlightened populace is created: citizens acquiring an ample vocabulary and extensive knowledge through indiscriminate reading—a process formerly known as a 'liberal education' (*'une tête bien faite'*)? Reading is an inoculation against dead language. Done with abandon, it can introduce the reader to unique word possibilities and new ideas, and offer a refuge from life's vagaries.

> "By far the most important thing to master is the use of metaphor. This is one thing that cannot be learnt from anyone else, and it is the mark of great natural ability, for the ability of metaphor implies a perception of resemblances."
>
> —Artistotle

Given that dead language—in its paper state—eradicates thousands of hectares of trees each year, shouldn't we call for a referendum to abolish it? Wouldn't our political representatives be eager to legislate the demise of the "politically correct" and terminologically opaque? Or not? Might we risk exposing ourselves to the following?

> The facts of the matter are these: There is no question that the issue of exanimate language is urgent and needs to be addressed at this time. With strategic planning and prudent procedures, our government, committed to staying the course in this era of global fiscal restraint, will manage this issue decisively as we move forward in building a diverse, sustainable, and prosperous society for generations to come. The Government of Canada intends to initiate legislation with clear

deadlines and fiscal responsibility which, when enacted, will bring forth wholesome verbal and written family prose, forming a pro-found language that will assist us to steward public expenditure, stimulate economic growth, protect our environment, celebrate our diverse aboriginal cultures, and support the valiant men and women of our armed forces. Most importantly, it will enable us to assist all Canadians to be themselves.

No. We cannot rely on these 'right honourable' men and women, the improvident politicians, who have neither the wit nor the imagination to rid themselves of dead rhetoric. It will be up to us to banish the 'speaks', honing every thought to its intended meaning in clear, vibrant, and plucky sentences.

2. Forms of Prose

The Undead Novel

Periodically, some wag writes an obituary for the novel, joyously reminiscing about its delights and mourning its demise. This ritual, which has transpired every twenty years or so over the past century (in these technologically driven times the occurrence seems almost daily), and which usually creates mild hysteria in what remains of the literary media.

But has the novel died? Walk into any large bookstore, and you will note browsers skulking among the tables, eyeing the books and bending down to whisper, "ain't you dead yet?" Yet, if the novel were dead, who could be writing and publishing these piles of prose?

Alex Barris, a writer who spent long years higgling with wily TV producers and publishers, told us once that "publishers drink the blood of authors from their skulls." On the other hand, the publishers we know feel that they put enormous effort into publishing a book on behalf of the writer who receives,

"What preserves the voices of the great authors from one century to the next is not the recording device (the clay tablet, the scroll, the codex, the book, the computer, the iPad) but the force of imagination and the power of expression. It is the strength of the words themselves, not their product placement, that invites the play of mind and induces a change of heart... I listen to anguished publishers tell sad stories about the disappearance of books and the death of Western civilization, about bookstores selling cat toys and teddy bears, but I don't find myself moved to tears... The renders of garments mistake the container for the thing contained, the book for the words, the iPod for the music. The questions in hand have to do with where the profit, not the meaning, is to be found, who collects what tolls from which streams of revenue... I know of no way out of what is the maze of the eternal present and the prison of self except with a string of words."

—Lewis Lapham,
Figures of Speech, Harper's

they believe, more than a fair return for their efforts. These opposing views indicate to us that the novel lives. For if it were dead, wouldn't all writers and publishers be on the street selling timeshares in Cancun condos, or panhandling? If the novel had died, wouldn't it mean that storytelling—an obsessive human activity—had perished as well? And yet, writers still write, publishers still publish, and storytelling flourishes. So the novel is not quite dead. It's been breathing since Don Quixote, and so continues.

In *The Art of the Novel*, Milan Kundera illustrates how the modern (European) novel evolved—from Miguel de Cervantes in the early seventeenth century to Franz Kafka in the twentieth century.

> "The first great novel, *Don Quixote*, teaches how the spiritual greatness, the boldness, the helpfulness, of one of the noblest of men, Don Quixote, are completely devoid of counsel and do not contain the slightest scintilla of wisdom."
>
> —Walter Benjamin, *The Storyteller: Reflections on the Works of Nikolai Leskov*

In *Don Quixote*, he suggests that the expanse of the setting—"Don Quixote set off into a world that opened wide before him"—opened up the sense of an endless landscape to the reader.

A century later, Diderot's two heroes in *Jacques le Fataliste* "exist in a time without beginning or end, in a space without frontiers, in the midst of a Europe whose future will never end." By Balzac, however, half a century on, "the distant horizon has disappeared like a landscape behind those modern structures, the social institutions: the police, the law, the world of money and crime, the army, the State."

And by *Madame Bovary*, "...the horizon shrinks to the point of seeming a barrier... The lost infinity of the outside world is replaced by the infinity of the soul" as "the great illusion of the irreplaceable uniqueness of the individual—one of Europe's finest illusions—blossoms forth."

Finally, this illusion is crushed in the early twentieth century, when Kafka piles the weight of "...history (or what remains of it: the supra human force of an omnipotent society)..." onto man and, in *The Trial* and *The Castle*, the soul's infinity has vanished in the oppression of those modern—now staunchly entrenched—complex social structures, resulting in an irretrievable loss of personal sovereignty.

Carlos Fuentes, in *Myself with Others,* sees that "...the modern age begins when Don Quixote de la Mancha, in 1605, leaves his village... and discovers that the world does not resemble what he has read about it. Many things are changing in the world; many others are surviving. *Don Quixote* tells us just this... how to accept the diversity and mutation of the world, while retaining the mind's power for analogy and unity, so that this changing world shall not become meaningless... *Don Quixote* [Cervantes] tells us that being modern is not a question of sacrificing the past in favor of the new, but of maintaining, comparing, and remembering values we have created, *making them modern so as not to lose the value of the modern."* [italics ours]

"Literature always anticipates life. It does not copy it, but moulds it to its purpose. The nineteenth century, as we know it, is largely an invention of Balzac."

—Oscar Wilde

"A novelist is a specialist in nothing... able to travel back and forth freely across the borders that demarcate disciplines. I can employ the concepts of science, the poetics of theology. I can speak as an anthropologist, a philosopher, a pornographer... I can resort to confession, autobiography, myths, legends, dreams, hallucinations, and the mutterings of poor mad people in the street."

—E.L. Doctorow,
Reporting the Universe

"Casting my mind's eye over the whole of fiction, the only absolutely original creation I can think of is Don Quixote."

—W. Somerset Maugham

Before the twentieth century, the novel, crammed with plot along with voluminous and effusive character and setting detail (in serialization, writers like Dickens were paid by the word), was the chief source of amusement for many middle- and upper-class Victorians. Yet, over the course of the twentieth century, modern media (radio, TV, Internet) supplanted its popularity. So, like a protozoan, it divided itself into genres—first into the western, detective, and sci-fi genres, and then into the fantasy, thriller, futuristic, gothic, allegorical, comic, erotic, paranormal, pornographic, magic realism, realism, post-realism, hyper-realism, picaresque, romance, gay, feminist, post-modern, reflective, satirical, stream of consciousness, utopian, dystopian, illustrated, and other genres—remaining, internationally, an assertive, cultural force.[1]

Stylistically, the twentieth-century novel grew more complex—along with the human condition. Although James Joyce himself suggested that, "The artist, like the God of creation, remains within or behind or beyond or above his handiwork, invisible, refined, out of existence, indifferent, paring his fingernails," it was Joyce who changed its path. After *Dubliners*

---

1. These genres come in many different languages. English novels (British, American, Canadian, Australian, etc.), Japanese, Russian, Egyptian, African, South African, Latin American, Chinese, Indian, French, German, Italian, Scandinavian, and many others. 110 countries published books in 2006, the total number of *books* published in 2006 is listed by UNESCO as over 1,900,000; but how many of these are novels? Google estimates that there are 129,864,880 books on Planet Earth—but again, how many are novels?

(1914), this anonymity disappeared and, in *A Portrait of an Artist as a Young Man, Ulysses,* and *Finnegan's Wake,* he saturated the narratives with his existence, creating a more labour-intensive relationship with the reader. That his influence was profound can be evidenced by the number of modern writers who eagerly followed his example.

In the recent past, the modern writer has been tempted to allow genre or style to dominate his or her prose. James Wood, in the *London Review of Books,* compared new translations of the work of Czech novelist Bohumil Hrabal (1915-1997) to: "... contemporary writers who are fond of abundant stories, exotic coloration, jokes and puns, and farcical escapism... we have lately encountered *terrorist groups with silly names, a genetically engineered mouse, two clocks having a conversation with each other, a giant cheese, a baby who plays air guitar in his crib* [italics ours] and so on."

Wood goes on to suggest that the reading public sees these 'imaginings' as creative, but astutely counsels "... *this is more like hysterical realism than magical realism: it borrows from the real while evading it* [italics ours]. These novels are profligate with what might be called inhuman stories: 'inhuman' not because they could never happen, but because they are not really about human beings. By

"No book worth its salt is meant to put you to sleep, it's meant to make you jump out of bed in your underwear and run and beat the author's brains out."

—Bohumil Hrabal,
Too Loud a Solitude

"...it would seem that the novel, with its common sense, is of all forms the least adapted to encompass the modern world, whose leading characteristic is irreality. And that, so far as I can understand, is why the novel is dying. The souped-up novels that are being written today, with injections of myth and symbols to heighten or 'deepen' the material, are simply evasions and forms of self-flattery."

—Mary McCarthy, *A Bolt from the Blue — The Fact is Fiction* contrast, Hrabal's magical stories are comic and human—they are really desires embodied."

What we take from Mr. Wood's overview is that genre or style shouldn't encumber the telling. If theme, narrative, voice, setting, characterization, dialogue, and syntax are present; if these are expressed fluently, simply, and imaginatively; and if the story is rooted in the human, it will arouse.

Plain prose makes it possible for the reader to willingly suspend disbelief, but if the writing is overwhelmed with spurious detail, heavy dialect, excessive description, or overly figurative speech, it's unlikely the reader will be able to enter the story. As George Orwell phrased it: "… one can write nothing readable unless one struggles constantly to efface one's personality. Good prose is like a window pane."

No, the novel is not dead. It still breathes, and our seduction by the visual—an addiction to screens big and small—has not signalled its death knell, yet. Much like the English language, the novel has shown a capacity to survive, to endure over centuries— and it still has the power to inspire, to reveal, to compel, to enchant, and to startle.

"The novel is the highest example of subtle interrelatedness that man has discovered."
—D.H. Lawrence

The Spellbinding Short Story

The short story, evolving from myth, fable, the Bible, Chaucer, Cervantes, Maupassant, Chekhov, and many other sources, can be gripping and revelatory—a streamlined work of art that, for an intense, short duration, can take us into a turbulent other world, which we leave with an altered perspective.

To accomplish this, the reader needs to be immediately inside the protagonist's dilemma. A short story is powerful because of its density and tension—eye of the storm—there's no time for vague, desultory description, the specific, animate details must be sharp, revealing ones, allowing us to enter right into the moment of conflict—to what's at stake.

"Any fiction should be a story. In any story there are three elements: persons, a situation, and the fact that in the end something has changed. If nothing has changed, it isn't a story."

— Malcolm Cowley,
The Paris Review

The following excerpt from Gabriella Goliger's short story, *Maedele,* in *Song of Ascent,* her evocative collection of stories centred on a Jewish family in Montreal, sits at the bottom of the first page, and pulls the reader into the protagonist's world immediately.

"Deception comes easily, perhaps because the truth is so preposterous, so slippery. She's been singled out by a great Yiddish poet, a visiting professor from Jerusalem. She is having an affair with a married man old enough to be her father. She's receiving private lessons from a Holocaust survivor who saw babies butchered, who was buried under corpses, who hid in a pit for almost two years. She is dreaming a B-grade movie where too much happens, a calamity a minute. She is dreaming corpses, she is falling into a pit, she is buried under a professor."

"A strick and succinct style is that, where you can take away nothing without loss, and that loss to be manifest."

—Ben Jonson

For those writers who read (and what interested and interesting writer doesn't?), any 'Best of...' short-story collections can prove instructive. After reading four or five collections, the differences and similarities in approach by various authors become apparent; and the

"Don't say it was 'delightful'; make us say 'delightful' when we've read the description. You see, all those words (horrifying, wonderful, hideous, exquisite) are only like saying to your readers 'Please will you do my job for me?'"

—C.S. Lewis

stories likely to remain with us are those that place us inside the protagonist's emotional reality right away. Effective stories are short on exposition, the authors slyly weaving in minute detail throughout the narrative.

Compelling short stories avoid: clusters of exposition, lack of inner or outer conflict (what's at stake?), incidents crammed with complicated syntax and detail, inaccurate wording, hyper-extended metaphors, and similes, all of which can kill the reader's interest.

> "An author in his work must be like God in the universe, present everywhere and visible nowhere."
>
> —Gustave Flaubert

In *Recommended Short Prose* [page 171], you will find a list of short stories—examples of intriguing prose—which illustrate a deft use of theme, narrative, voice, setting, characterization, dialogue, and syntax. These tales hook the reader immediately and propel them through the narrative at great velocity. Impressionistic in form, the short story is a unique mode for illuminating the emotional, psychological and philosophical molecules that lurk in the human psyche.

The Absorbing Memoir

> "A memoir is how one remembers one's own life, while an autobiography is history, requiring research, dates, facts double-checked. I've taken the memoir route on the ground that even an idling memory is apt to get right what matters most."
>
> —Gore Vidal, *Palimpsest*

A recent biography of a revered Canadian political leader had the effect of dulling this great and colourful man's life to an inert grey. The author *explained* the subject's life but didn't *show* it, using almost no anecdotes or revealing details, frustrating the curious reader who wanted to discover what had made this intensely fearless individual tick. What animates a memoir, autobiography, or biography is the flotsam and jetsam of that life illustrated by specific animate detail of people and events as well as moments that reveal the subject's humanity, fears and desires—the life forces that formed their personalities, and to which the reader can relate.

Describing the life rather than *showing* it doesn't allow the reader to understand it. If the biographer backs away from the 'warts and all' approach, he or she discards the very human traits that allow us to grasp the raison d'être of the subject's life. The memoirist or biographer needs anecdote and detail and the basic elements of prose to bring the subject to life. If any of these elements are missing, the body will lie bloodless on the page.

> "All slang is metaphor, and all metaphor is poetry."
> —G.K. Chesterton

The Forceful Screenplay

A commanding screenplay requires a strong narrative line—the movies you remember (e.g. THE THIRD MAN, CITIZEN KANE, THE GODFATHER, MIDNIGHT COWBOY, ON THE WATERFRONT, THE BICYCLE THIEF, etc.) all contain an imperative story. Although *character, dialogue,* and *setting* might appear to be the most visible elements, *narrative* lies just beneath the surface, binding the others.

Theme and *voice* support *narrative* (even sometimes carrying it, e.g. APOCALYPSE NOW, SUNSET BOULEVARD), and any writer who can effectively utilize all three can concoct an irresistible screen story. Yet, if it's that easy, why are so many mediocre pictures made?

In the picture business, two groups dominate: the ones who know HOW TO MAKE PICTURES, and the ones who KNOW HOW TO GET PICTURES MADE—both locked in a struggle for creative control, both lacking the other's talent. Those who know HOW TO MAKE PICTURES (screenwriters and directors) lack the money-thugness of mind required to get one made, while those who know HOW TO GET PICTURES MADE (producers) lack the imagination to make one (few comprehend the difference between 'laughing at the characters' and 'laughing with the characters'). Each needs the other; and when that's understood, transformative pictures are often the result.

This can present difficulties for the screenwriter who is caught between the two: the eager, unaware ones, driven mad by the perpetual input of unoriginal ideas from those who know HOW TO GET PICTURES MADE, either adapt, quit, or turn psychotic; the canny ones, treading lightly, attempt surreptitiously to slip substance into the work.

The screenwriter needs to remember that without words on paper, there is no picture, as revealed by an apocryphal story from 1930s Hollywood. Émigré director Ernst Lubitsch, having endowed a series of successful, sophisticated comedies with the "Lubitsch Touch," was being honoured at a dinner. As the tale goes, a seasoned screenwriter arrived at the dais, held up a screenplay consisting of blank pages, stared at Lubitsch in the front row and said, "put the 'Lubitsch Touch' on this."

Producers who insist on being 'creatively involved' unknowingly place a burden on their projects, especially before it has crystallized in the mind of the writer, who is attempting to approach the work with his or her imagination unfettered. The astute screenwriter, listening to all suggestions from the money side—most of which will appear feckless—will focus on a search for potential story fragments.

Those who know HOW TO GET PICTURES MADE will want to cram their movies with 'events' large enough to excite the most indiscriminating of viewers: a car speeding, flipping over onto its roof and exploding; horses running off a cliff; or, if the budget is large enough, an avalanche or an earthquake. These 'action' events, however, can never equal the empathy a vulnerable screen character can transmit to an audience.

In the late 1960s, the success of pictures like BONNIE AND CLYDE and THE GRADUATE, and particularly of EASY RIDER, a low-budget, independent, contemporary film, indicated a trickle of substance infiltrating the Hollywood system. Producers, aware now that movies with a 'down' ending and three-dimensional characters could generate profit, began to seek out scripts with strong subject matter.

Subsequently, in the early 1970s, pictures like SHAMPOO, CHINATOWN, MIDNIGHT COWBOY, MEAN STREETS, ONE FLEW OVER THE CUCKOO'S NEST, PAPER MOON, THE LAST PICTURE SHOW, ANNIE HALL, TAXI DRIVER, FIVE EASY PIECES, A CLOCKWORK ORANGE,

"The efficiency of the thriller genre takes just what it needs from the much less efficient Flaubert or Isherwood, and throws away what made those writers truly alive. And of course, the most economically privileged genre of this kind of largely lifeless 'realism' is commercial cinema, through which most people nowadays receive their idea of what constitutes a 'realistic' narrative."

—James Wood,
How Fiction Works

[Hollywood] "A dreary industrial town controlled by hoodlums of enormous wealth, the ethical sense of a pack of jackals, and taste so degraded that it befouled everything it touched."

—S.J. Perelman,
The Paris Review

and M.A.S.H., released to a movie public hungry for content, gave the impression that film would again challenge theatre and fiction as an art form, as it had at its birth.

Nope.

In the late 1970s, two occurrences signalled the end of this renaissance. The first, the unimaginable financial success of STAR WARS (1977), a sci-fi movie by George Lucas, demonstrated that simplistic story elements (two-dimensional characters) in exotic locales (outer space), reminiscent of earlier action movies (spaceship combat scenes modelled on actual combat scenes from World War II movies), could reap millions.

"Hollywood money isn't money. It's congealed snow, melts in your hand, and there you are. I can't talk about Hollywood. It was a horror to me when I was there and it's a horror to look back on... Once I was coming down a street in Beverly Hills and I saw a Cadillac about a block long, and out of the side window was a wonderfully slinky mink, and an arm, and at the end of the arm a hand in a white suede glove wrinkled around the wrist, and in the hand was a bagel with a bite out of it."

—Dorothy Parker,
The Paris Review

The second occurrence was the publication of *Screenplay* (1979) by Syd Field, a set of mechanical rules for writing screenplays, which focused on technique rather than narrative and process.

Field's book (which was popular with those who know HOW TO GET PICTURES MADE) promoted a pedantic, left-brain approach to screenwriting, ignoring the turbulent possibilities that hover on the edge of the imagination—those plot-less glimmers of the right brain—stressing instead the need (before beginning the screenplay) to detail all story elements (i.e. plot points), and outline entire histories for the characters.

Disagreeing with Kurt Vonnegut's view of art and life as "a series of random moments," Field insisted that life was but a continuum of beginnings, middles, and ends (just like in the movies), reinforcing Gore Vidal's wry observation that all Hollywood movies end with a wedding. Ironically, *Screenplay's* prose—repetitive, with no telling anecdote or detail—is ponderous. More readable, and knowledgeable, is *On Writing*, Stephen King's pertinent thoughts on storytelling, the basis of any well-made screenplay (as verified by the many Stephen King books made into movies).

Although these offerings led the way to the current creative stasis in Hollywood (within the dumbing-down of late twentieth-century America), neither Lucas nor Field can be blamed for the mediocrity, or mendacity, of contemporary Hollywood movie-making. The truth is simpler—business trumps creativity, and a movie executive with an MBA is far less likely (unlike their predecessors, i.e., Thalberg, Goldwyn, etc.) to understand how good pictures get made than one with a degree in the humanities.

> "Hollywood is like being nowhere and talking to nobody about nothing."
>
> — Michelangelo Antonioni

So where does this leave the earnest screenwriter? Novelist Graham Greene, who crafted film scripts first in story form (e.g. *The Third Man*)—or simply got on with writing the novel before attempting the screenplay—tells us in *Ways of Escape*, "To me it is almost impossible to write a film play without first writing a story. *Even a film depends on more than plot, on a certain measure of characterization, on mood and atmosphere;* and these seem to me almost impossible to capture for the first time *in the dull shorthand of a script...* one

"So many people, from Lenin and Chaplin to Zuckerberg and Jobs, have believed that moving imagery on screens might unify and enlighten the world. Isn't it pretty to think so? The screen has also distanced us; it has made us feel powerless, helpless, and not there. The array of watching devices that have swept over "cinema" in the last thirty years will accelerate and spread, and of course they are helpful and profitable—just look at the economy they have produced. Might they also be the lineaments of a coming fascism? Don't be alarmed, it will be much more polite or user-friendly than the clumsy version of the 1930s, but as deadening as the shopping malls of Americana, the nullity of so many of its schools, the unending madness of its advertising, and the stony indifference of technology."
—David Thomson, *The Big Screen*

must have the sense of more material than one needs to draw on." [italics ours]

Stirling Silliphant, a prolific movie and TV writer, in an interview that appeared in the original *The Screenwriter Looks at the Screenwriter* (published in 1972 by William Froug), suggested eliminating the scene headers that facilitate script breakdowns, freeing the screenwriter to focus on narrative. Instead of EXT – NIGHT – RIVER, he thought it more evocative to begin a scene with a line of prose (e.g. "the blue moonlight threw Evelyn's shadow across the river"). From that description and the scene, the production manager would know the location, time of day, props and actors needed, etc., allowing the actors and director to be enveloped in the emotional reality of the scene). To Mr. Silliphant, being part of the breakdown process represented creative restraint, which might be why screenwriters often feel like mechanics and not magicians.

Take hope, screenwriter. There are still a few intelligent producers who understand the utility of a well-crafted screenplay. Given the vagaries of the movie business, the odds are long against your meaningful script being produced. However, there is the chance that it will be read, possibly optioned, and you might be offered other projects to write (for money), enabling you to continue working on your novel.

The Other Prose

While this book is primarily concerned with fiction and biography, *theme, narrative, voice, setting, character, dialogue,* and *syntax* affect every form of expository prose (e.g. in theatrical plays a strong narrative is essential). A history such as *Blood and Daring* by John Boyko, a depiction of Canada's Confederation as engendered by the American Civil War, is compelling reading *because* Boyko is adept at utilizing all those elements.

Poetry—not considered prose, except for the prose poem—benefits as well. Many poems appear as clusters of incompatible word images, but with *theme, narrative,* and *voice,* and the addition of *setting, characterization, dialogue,* and *syntax* used well, this form can astonish. Many of the best-known modern poetic works contain all these elements: *Leaves of Grass,* Walt Whitman; *Innisfree,* W.B. Yeats; *I Sing of Olaf,* e.e. cummings; *Fern Hill* and *A Refusal to Mourn the Death by Fire of a Child in London,* Dylan Thomas; *Howl,* Allen Ginsberg.

> "If I feel physically that the top of my head were taken off, I know that it is poetry."
> —Emily Dickinson

3. The Elements of Prose

Theme — Have You Got One?

Gore Vidal used to relate the story of Bryce, a best-selling, first-time novelist who, over the years, had produced no other work. He had partied, dawdled and dallied, letting his talent wither. One morning, lying in bed, his head pained by alcohol consumed the night before, he had a vision of his second novel—and it was monumental, a work finally worthy of his immense talent, a theme so exalted that, upon completion, it would at once restore his reputation. Such a saga, however, could be told only in a trilogy, the titles of which came to him as if in a vision. He rose with fresh purpose, showered and, to bolster his courage as he shaved, declaimed the three titles to the mirror: "*The Plains, The Mountains and The Sea*." Bryce, however, was onto himself. He stared wistfully at his reflection for a moment and added, "A trilogy-wilogy by Brycey Whycey."

"Unprovided with original learning, unformed in the habits of thinking, unskilled in the arts of composition, I resolved to write a book."

—Edward Gibbon

"The main characters in a novel must necessarily have some kinship to the author, they come out of his body as a child comes from the womb, then the umbilical cord is cut, and they grow into independence. The more the author knows of his own character the more he can distance himself from his invented characters and the more room they have to grow in."

—Graham Greene,
Ways of Escape

The sad tale of Bryce illustrates the confusion that befuddles writers who wait for a worthwhile theme to occur to them. As Artie Shaw noted, 'time is all you got' and, as no one wants to risk it on a subject of little consequence, the search is endless: What *is* a serious and worthwhile theme? Is it one that reveals a universal truth? Or could it have something to do with that insignificant incident or embarrassing situation plaguing my memory? Will it touch the reader? Will it lead to a narrative, and will it be worth the weeks, months, and years I spend trying to get it down? The theme-search of a previously best-selling novelist like Bryce is driven by the desire to *remain* a best-seller, but that's rarely a problem for the rest of us.

"A novel is never anything but a philosophy put into images."
—Albert Camus

"The real comic novel has to do with man's recognition of his unimportance in the universe."
—Anthony Burgess

People who write because they're obsessed usually have a vague idea of what they want to say—a compulsion that sits in the back of their thoughts, consciously or unconsciously colouring the narrative. In *The Horse That Leaps Through Clouds,* by Eric Enno Tamm, what first appears as an enthralling travelogue—the author in 2006 reconstructing an overland journey from Moscow to Peking made by a Russian spy in 1906—at book's end is revealed to be a sly rumination on the political state of China. Having led the reader safely from Moscow to Beijing, Tamm asks us to ponder the modern history of Chinese governance.

Finding A Theme

The writer doesn't wake one morning and declare, "Today, I will write about Man's inhumanity to Man." The story (with a theme lurking in the subconscious) will trickle out, with questioning:

i)   What concerns me? What are my dreams telling me? What gives me hope? What touches me? What makes me laugh or cry?

ii)   What terrifies me—apathy, environmental degradation, medical malfeasance, the response to autism and PTSD, chronic or fatal ailments, mental illness, pop culture, etc.?

iii) What exactly is the human condition—are we decent or mean and rapacious? Is existence beautiful or horrifying or both? Does living life to the full bring trouble or joy? Will a solitary monk achieve tranquillity and peace or loneliness? Which is more appropriate, an eye for an eye or turn the other cheek? What are we all searching for? Is this my place in the natural order of things? Etc.

iv)   Does a theme need to be earth-shattering? Or is it a microcosm of a larger problem or issue? (When Günter

"Traditionally, the virtuous member of the middle class is encouraged to cultivate sincerity and its twin, hypocrisy. The sort of harsh truth-telling that one gets in Aristophanes, say, is not possible in a highly organized zoo like the United States where the best cuts are flung to those who never question the zoo's management. The satirist breaks with his origins; looks at things with a cold eye; says what he means, and mocks those who do not know what *they* mean."

—Gore Vidal, "Thomas Love Peacock: the Novel of Ideas", *United States: Essays 1952-1992*

"Everything has been said before, but since nobody listens we have to keep going back and beginning all over again."

— André Gide

Grass was approached by Kurt Wolff in 1962 to publish *The Tin Drum* in America, Grass suggested that his novel, set in Gdansk, might be too "provincial." Wolff replied, "All great literature is rooted in the provincial.")

v)   Should I approach this work as a short story, novel, play, or poem?

vi)   If it's personal will it engage *any* reader?

vii)   Do I present the theme overtly or covertly? Should it 'stalk' the reader?

viii)   What's at stake in my narrative? How do I convey it without appearing to proselytize?

ix)   What's driving me to set it down? Can I spend two years (or more) of my life writing and rewriting what might turn out to be a pile of self-absorbed musings (crap)?

The writer needs to trust that, in pondering all these questions, the answers will appear—when they're ready. What he or she is hoping to do is to start the engine—to plant a seed in the subconscious, which usually begins with an image that intrigues. If that sprouts a story fragment, it might then blossom into a series of incidents: the larva stage of theme. A concrete word (e.g. trousers, filet, algae, bra, skillet, dairy, cricket, egg, dupe, garage, heifer, plimsoll, intestine, libretto, knoll, joist, zoot suit, stew, pedestal, mohair, node, etc.) can often spark an image which could lead to a character, on to an incident, and finally to the beginnings of a narrative.

The writer, fumbling to find a narrative to support the theme—or groping to find the theme that threads the story—might write many pages in which nothing happens. Often, these meanderings will lead to an incident and then to a change or shift. Suddenly, after pages of nothing happening, something happens—a change—what the writer intended to write but didn't consciously know how. And that change might suggest a theme, and provide a psychological framework from within which she or he can flesh out the narrative. Then, by omitting the meanderings in the rewrite, the story is tightened until it's taut.

Writers who have difficulty in coming up with *any* ideas at all might try to spring one loose by:

i) sitting at the computer / desk every day and doodling for an hour—writing anything that comes to mind. Eventually, a word fragment might suggest an image, which might lead to a scene, which could generate a narrative linė, and even possibly a theme;

ii) 'what iffing':
- *What if* I were on holiday in a hotel in Cairo and spotted someone who looked like Osama bin Laden / Saddam

> "Originality is nothing but judicious imitation. The most original writers borrowed from one another. The instruction we find in books is like fire. We fetch it from our neighbours, kindle it at home, communicate it to others, and it becomes the property of all."
> —Voltaire

> "To a chemist, nothing on earth is unclean. A writer must be as subjective... he must abandon the subjective line; he must know that dungheaps play a very respectable part in a landscape, and that evil passions are as inherent in life as good ones."
> —Anton Chekhov

> "Ideas are like rabbits. You get a couple and learn how to handle them, and pretty soon you have a dozen."
> —John Steinbeck

Hussein / Muammar al-Gaddafi / George W. Bush, etc. smoking a joint on the next balcony?

- *What if* a catastrophically large iceberg (i.e. ten square kilometres) hit the coast of Newfoundland just offshore from my summer cottage and a boy of ten—my son— was the person trapped on the ice?

- *What if* my mother was elected to public office, and a news publication revealed that her past life as a prostitute had produced a son or daughter—me—and I discovered that my father was a mafioso, an ex-spy, etc.?

"A species living under the threat of obliteration is bound to produce obliterature,— and that's what we are producing."

—James Thurber

- *What if* a man, convinced that his children will die as a result of climate change, began to attack all automobiles with I.E.D.s, and plot the assassination of pro-fossil-fuel CEOs and politicians?

- *What if* a young boy, distraught at watching ducks dying in a toxic tar sands tailings pond on the news, made his way to northern Alberta to save them?

- *What if* a man, enraged by usage charges on his monthly internet bill, and frustrated with yelling at call centre employees in distant countries, attempted to embarrass (or kill) the CEO at a shareholders' meeting?

"I think that to write well and convincingly, one must be somewhat poisoned by emotion. Dislike, displeasure, resentment, fault-finding, imagination, passionate remonstrance, a sense of injustice— they all make fine fuel."

—Edna Ferber

A piece of prose is a platform, a dream or nightmare, an idea, a device that allows you to vent, to analyse, to reflect, to amuse, to construct or reconstruct, possibly to effect change—an attempt to share your point of view with others.

> "The man who writes for fools is always sure of a large audience."
>
> —Arthur Schopenhauer

Here in the early twenty-first century, we live 'in interesting times' (according to the Chinese blessing). Life on Planet Earth is increasingly fast-paced, competitive, complex, and confusing; writing—a tool for psychological survival—might reveal meaning beneath its surface. If writers write what they see and feel, they will experience a sense of bending with the wind in an ungovernable world. If what troubles us affects others, our prose might find an audience—or not—but we will have increased our knowledge of the world and our place in it. We read and write to feel less alone.

Self-doubt is part of the process, the weight an artist carries, as he or she struggles forward, demanding hard answers to difficult questions. The tales are legion of gifted writers and painters destroying their manuscripts and canvases—and themselves—in fits of despair. This obsessive form of artistic integrity—eradicating creations that do not live up to the benchmark set by the artist—could be defined as self-flagellation. It's useful to remember that self-flagellation and self-doubt are not the same. Self-doubt drives us forward, makes us think harder and deeper. Self-flagellation annihilates us.

> "All of old. Nothing else ever. Ever tried. Ever failed. No matter. Try again. Fail again. Fail better."
>
> —Sam Beckett

Whatever theme you've chosen for your work, ask yourself:

i)   Does it deal with something that matters deeply to me, some piece of the human puzzle which will also absorb the reader?

ii)   Is it a theme which I believe will be worth spending time exploring—even if I fail?

iii) Is it a theme which readily provides a *narrative*?

Narrative = Incidence + Character

Narrative has been with us since the early hunter-gatherers. Before and during Homer's day (circa 750 B.C.), epic poetry (the stories of the battles of great kings and queens) was composed orally, memorized, and spread—not on paper or papyrus or tablets—by male rhapsodes (professional reciters) who declaimed them as they wandered through the ancient world. Although the scribes of earlier civilizations had been able to preserve their stories, the Greeks did so only later.

> "What is wrong with writing today [1986] is its flaccidity, its lack of pleasure in the manipulation of sounds and pauses. The written word is becoming inert. One dreads to think what it will be like in 2020."
>
> —Anthony Burgess

Memorizing verse over the past two millennia has been a beneficial activity in all societies, particularly in schools. The belief that narrative (and rhyming) strengthens memory is verified by research into the brain—another reason why prose and poetry are useful to humans. (It's impossible to imagine a 'rhapsode' using twitter, a technology limited to 140 characters.)

We know very little about Homer, or *The Iliad* and *The Odyssey*. From ancient history, we do know that these extended verse narratives were based on actual events, but we don't know if Homer wrote them (or if the 'writing' was memorized only), or if they were created (or embellished) by others. If he did compose them, how much license did he

> "[Writing]'s like driving a car at night. You never see further than your headlights, but you can make the whole trip that way."
>
> —E. L. Doctorow

take in the telling? And how was he able to generate, manage, and retain huge narratives—fully fleshed out—without the use of pen and paper? To conceive and remember narratives of that length without writing them down would require a very supple mind. Once fabricated, were they rewritten? If so, how? Homer's achievement is even more majestic placed against the analogy made by E. L. Doctorow.

If we extend Doctorow's simile to include the reader, it encompasses the totality of the experience of literature—the writer is in the driver's seat, peering ahead through the windshield at the darkness, trying to glimpse the narrative; the reader is in the passenger seat, intently watching the writer, until finally she or he is staring ahead, aware only of the narrative.

"What is character but the determination of incident? What is incident but the illustration of character?"

—Henry James

Narrative is formed by incidents (large or small) which connect the story from beginning to end—incidents centred around a protagonist and an antagonist who hold our interest, have motives or personality traits capable of precipitating events, and who try to overcome some obstacle or achieve some goal.

This might seem demanding, especially with a story that relies not on exterior incidents but on conflict within the protagonist. With a novel, the constant pull on the writer's imagination is daunting; you might spend years staring at the screen or paper each day, mapping out your narrative, willing it to move forward.

The narrative should allow the reader to *eagerly suspend his or her disbelief*; but, to captivate, the writer needs to reveal immediately the characters' dilemma while remaining within the boundaries of credibility—the reader should never stop to wonder where she or he is. A flying saucer landing outside a saloon in the middle of a Western novel would remove the reader from the narrative because it beggars belief. The narrative needs to unfold within *parameters*—and always with something at stake.

There are, of course, exceptions—proving the rule. Two well-known novels, *The Master and Margarita* and *Tristram Shandy*, both taunt the reader by flouting the rules; Bulgakov with *The Master and Margarita* asks the reader to willing suspend disbelief when he has the Devil visit Moscow in the mid-twentieth century without convincingly (to us) motivating Satan's sudden appearance.

With *Tristram Shandy*, rather than try to efface all signs of the author, Sterne flaunts himself on every page, digressing, continually gulling the reader as he or she searches in vain for the narrative. Part of what seems odd about the success of these two fictions is that neither novel appears to have an emotional centre. Yet, inexplicably, both books have many admirers, and remain in print.

> "... whereas an aptitude for mathematics or physics is given to relatively few, narrative seems to be within everyone's grasp, perhaps because it was the very first means people ever had to understand who they were and what was happening to them."
>
> —E.L. Doctorow,
> *Reporting the Universe*

> "Forward motion in any piece of writing is carried by verbs. Verbs are the action words of the language and the most important. Turn to any passage on any page of a successful novel and notice the high percentage of verbs. Beginning writers always use too many adjectives and adverbs and generally use too many dependent clauses."
>
> —William Sloane

Creating a Narrative Line

i)   In his short story, *Korea*, John McGahern has an Irish father try to convince his son to go to America. In mid-story, the son discovers that his parents have learned that a neighbour's son, serving with the U.S. Army in Korea, was killed in action and, as a result, the soldier's parents were awarded ten thousand dollars (American military policy during the Korean War). McGahern must have started with this fact and then created the premise of a coming-of-age Irish lad with dim family prospects reacting to the discovery that his death represented a potential source of income to his parents. McGahern uses this fact to illustrate the complicated relationships between parents and offspring, and how such a revelation might bring a young man to understand that his youth is over.

> "When I used to teach writing, I would tell my students to make their characters want something right away--even if it's only a glass of water. Characters paralysed by the meaninglessness of modern life still have to drink water from time to time."
>
> —Kurt Vonnegut

> "A man may write at any time, if he will set himself doggedly to it."
>
> —Samuel Johnson

ii)   Once the writer has a premise or a fact, it might be accompanied by a character who could then be connected to an incident, an action, or a conflict. The incident may not be essential—and might be discarded in the rewrites—but it allows the story to begin. With each incident added, the narrative will ramble but grow. Eventually, by cutting away incidents that don't support the storyline, the arc of the narrative will emerge.

> "When the characters are really alive before their author, the latter does nothing but follow them in their action, in their words, in the situations they suggest to him."
>
> —Luigi Pirandello

iii)   Keep questioning. Does the narrative have 'guts'? Does it move fast enough to keep the reader on edge? Is it engaging?

iv)   Try not to walk the reader through the story. Take chances. The less linear the narrative, the more the reader will be intrigued, provided it remains taut and the *voice* is strong. The reader has to sense that the writer won't drive the story off the road or let it stall.

v)   A ***Novel*** requires a more complex narrative than a short story. In creating it, you can take comfort in Doctorow's words, taking it one incident at a time. As you wend your way through a first draft, your imagination will keep bounding ahead, generating new story chunks. Let it. All breathtaking prose is initially serendipity, and you might arrive at a much different location than you had envisioned. Your story might have been gestating in the nether reaches of your mind for some time, gushing out as soon as you attempt to express it—your subconscious working overtime.

> "Writing a book is a horrible, exhausting struggle, like a long bout of some painful illness. One would never undertake such a thing if one were not driven by some demon whom one can neither resist nor understand. For all one knows that demon is the same instinct that makes a baby squall for attention. And yet it is also true that one can write nothing readable unless one constantly struggles to efface one's personality. Good prose is like a windowpane."
>
> —George Orwell

In the likely event that you end up staring at the screen or paper knowing that something has to happen but not knowing what, go what-iffing. *What if* this happens, *what if* that happens? *Something* has to happen.

vi)   A ***Short Story*** is usually focused on a single incident that effects a change, an element or occurrence that

"In ancient times, presumably, the storyteller got a spot near the fire because the story he told defined the powers to which the listener was subject and suggested how to live with them. Literature was as valuable as a club or a sharpened bone. It bound the present to the past, the visible with the invisible, and it helped to compose the community necessary for the continuing life of its members."

—E.L. Doctorow,
Jack London, Hemingway and the Constitution

presents a change to the life (or lives) of the character(s). Contemporary short stories tend to keep pace with trends in society, but many now seem to lack that necessary physical, emotional, or psychological change. *Character* and *setting* might be present, but that *something at stake*—driving the narrative—is often missing. Conflict creates friction, energy, and narrative drive. If you've jotted down a few pages describing a walk you and your boy / girlfriend took around the block and what you observed, it's not enough to note interesting characters and settings. A change must transpire: to you, the boy / girlfriend, or to someone you met on that walk. If nothing happened, it's not a story. In all prose, the reader needs to feel something's at stake, and that a physical, emotional, or psychological change is imminent. We crave that 'eureka' moment, that sudden understanding of what the story is about and why we read it—not the mounting disappointment of a non-narrative meandering to an inconclusive finish. Imagine a gathering of Palaeolithic primitives around a fire one night, eagerly listening to the tale-teller describe his walk into the forest, seeing trees and a mammoth, then returning to the cave. Those cavemen and women, expecting a story—with a change, an insight, a revelation, or a dramatic denouement—and not hearing one, would have stoned the tale-teller.

Although the short-story landscape is not as vast as the novel's, the impact of the change isn't necessarily less. Short stories tend to be impressionistic, less plot-driven than novels, but the change in a short story—interior or exterior, physical, mental, emotional— has the potential to be more immediate than that of a novel, its narrative more dynamic to ensure maximum impact. Hemingway, when asked to write a short story in one sentence, replied, "For sale, baby shoes, never used."

> "One wants to tell a story, like Scheherazade, in order not to die. It's one of the oldest urges of mankind. It's a way of stalling death."
> —Carlos Fuentes

vii) In a **Screenplay**, a strong narrative is essential, even in an action film, which usually comes with more plot events and twists than a story centred on character, dealing with interior changes. It's a step-by-step process—the screenwriter creating a map to allow the director and actors to work their way through the emotional minefields leading to the climax.

viii) Much depends on narrative in a **Memoir** or **Biography**, and other forms of non-fiction. For a reader to close a memoir before the last page might indicate the omission of revealing incident *in the writing*, not necessarily in the life. Even with all the other elements of prose present (e.g. *voice*, setting, etc.), a strong *narrative* animates the subject. A strong *theme* helps, linking the life-defining incidents. Love of subject—reflected in specific, animate detail and anecdotes that reveal the subject firmly in his or her time—is

> "When you put down the good things you ought to have done, and leave out the bad things you did do, that's memoirs."
> —Will Rogers

also key, which is what makes *The Life of Samuel Johnson* by Boswell one of the great biographies. Being able to reveal the daily struggle of the subject within his or her time is essential. Two remarkable memoirs are Rousseau's *Confessions,* and *Autobiography* by Benvenuto Cellini, both keen examples of the 'unreliable narrator,' and both vividly revealing the era in which they were written, as well as their love of subject.

ix)   *Narrative* also applies to poetry. Without it and *voice* and *theme*, a **Poem** will likely resemble a collection of random word-images thrown onto the page. To engage, a poem especially requires a *narrative*—the revealed incidents that keep us reading—to lasso those frisky metaphors and similes.

> "Buffoons and poets are near related and willingly seek each other out."
>
> —Johann Wolfgang von Goethe

To reiterate, a non-droopy *narrative* is lean, tying all events together, pulling readers through the story—secure in the knowledge that they will arrive at a destination.

Often, *Narrative* is given a boost with *Voice.*

Voice – Who's Telling the Story?

The opening of *The Third Policeman*, Flann O'Brien's extraordinary journey into a comic Irish netherworld, uses a compelling First Person voice to whack the reader into the *narrative*.

"Not everybody knows how I killed old Phillip Mathers, smashing his jaw in with my spade; but first it is better to speak of my friendship with John Divney because it was he who first knocked old Mathers

down by giving him a great blow in the neck with a special bicycle-pump which he manufactured himself out of a hollow iron bar. Divney was a strong civil man but he was lazy and idle-minded. He was personally responsible for the whole idea in the first place. It was he who told me to bring my spade. He was the one who gave the orders on the occasion and also the explanations when they were called for."

> "A book begins as an image, a sound in the ear, the haunting of something you don't want to remember, or perhaps a great endowing anger. But it is not until you find a voice for whatever is going on inside you that you can begin to make a coherent composition."
>
> —E.L. Doctorow, *Reporting the Universe*

The mindset of O'Brien's protagonist is only one of the delights of this startling narrative. For example, do we know if the narrator is telling the truth? He seems to shift all the blame in Divney's direction; and then there's the matter of the "special bicycle pump which he [Divney] manufactured himself out of a hollow iron bar." Is it possible for a "lazy and idle-minded" man to do this? Could the narrator be mendacious or deluded?

Of all the elements essential for creating astringent prose, *Voice* (aside from narrative) is possibly the most influential. When you remember the novels you've loved, undoubtedly what you remember is the tone of storytelling that drew you into the narrative.

Voice is that fascinating stranger you've just met who tells you his or her story, and who gives the reader an intimate glimpse of people he or she once knew. A strong voice is

> "The author must keep his mouth shut when his work starts to speak."
>
> —Friedrich Wilhelm Nietzsche

dependent on acute observation of human nature, and the author's being able to add a sense of urgency and tension to the telling.

The basic voice or Point of View (POV) possibilities are:

First Person "I," "we" – the voice telling you its own story, or one to which it is directly or tangentially connected. Novels such as: *Moby Dick, The Catcher in the Rye, David Copperfield, Brideshead Revisited, The Ginger Man* (with the narrator occasionally offering a glimpse of Third Person Subjective), *Huckleberry Finn, Gulliver's Travels, The Third Man, The Sun Also Rises, Of Human Bondage, Wide Sargasso Sea, The Quiet American* and *The Tin Drum* are all written in First Person— someone relating his or her story—with an intimacy that pulls the reader in immediately. *The Book of Laughter and Forgetting* and *Slaughterhouse Five* are curious but effective mixtures of First Person and Third Person Omniscient.

> "To write in the first person seems the easiest. As all young journal-writers assume. Actually it may be the hardest—there are so many hazards. Garrulity. Lack of shape, or proportion. Or even of judgment. On the other hand, when you're really riding that horse well, it can feel as if you're on Bucephalus. And you really feel the wind on you."
>
> —Hortense Calisher,
> *The Paris Review*

Second Person "you" – the voice addressing the reader directly, as though the reader were a character in the story—sometimes, *it* is another character in the story. Prose stories in this voice are rare, aside from *Winnie the Pooh* and *The House at Pooh Corner*, which appear to be written in Second Person and Third Person Omniscient. The short story *Dead Girls* by Nancy Lee is an example of a story written in Second Person. (Note: Much of this book is written in Second Person, addressing you, the reader).

Third Person Subjective "he/she/they" – the voice telling the reader the story of a particular character from that character's POV only, used in novels such as *Candide, Sentimental*

Education, 1984, Alice's Adventures in Wonderland, Lost Illusions, The Chrysalids, A Handful of Dust, and *Silas Marner.*

Third Person Omniscient – the voice as a central intelligence, taking an overview, and telling the story at will from several characters' POVs (as in Tolstoy, Chekhov, or Austen). Examples include novels such as: *Lady Chatterley's Lover, Catch 22, Pride and Prejudice* (or any Jane Austen novel), *Brave New World, Don Quixote, Brighton Rock, Middlemarch, Ulysses, Madame Bovary, Nostromo, Winnie the Pooh, The Loved One, Wind in the Willows, Day of the Locust,* and *The Grapes of Wrath.*

Any fragment of overheard conversation, incident, or text has the potential to trigger a story and, if we're lucky, arrives with a *voice*. A voice can come from anywhere—friends, family, the media, the office, the streets, the subway, the coffee shop, etc. Often, the writer can build an entire story from a quirky fragment but, in extending it into something longer (i.e. a novella or a novel), will need to maintain consistency so that the reader remains caught by the voice.

The writer might find, having started with one voice, that it's impossible to sustain for an entire novel. Rather than jettison the work up to that point, let the characters interact to see if that suggests an alternate voice. If it does, see if that voice can sustain First, Second or Third Person Subjective or Omniscient for an entire novel and—if it seems possible—consider changing the voice. Usually, the voice will choose the author, not the reverse.

Often, in First Person, the story is told from the POV of a peripheral character rather than that of the protagonist, adding mystery to the protagonist. The device of an onlooker divulging the story (e.g. *The Great Gatsby, All the King's Men, The Third Man*) allows the writer to disclose the protagonist's plight incrementally, and to build and heighten dramatic or comedic tension. The onlooker is used frequently not only in novels and short stories but in movies as well.

> *Moby Dick* – "Call me Ishmael. Some years ago—never mind how long precisely—having little or no money in my purse, and nothing particular to interest me on shore, I thought I would sail about a little and see the watery part of the world. It is a way I have of driving off the spleen and regulating the circulation. Whenever I find myself growing grim about the mouth; whenever it is a damp, drizzly November in my soul; whenever I find myself involuntarily pausing before coffin warehouses, and bringing up the rear of every funeral I meet; and especially whenever my hypos get such an upper hand of me, that it requires a strong moral principle to prevent me from deliberately stepping into the street, and methodically knocking people's hats off—then, I account it high time to get to sea as soon as I can. This is my substitute for pistol and ball. With a philosophical flourish Cato throws himself upon his sword; I quietly take to the ship. There is nothing surprising in this. If they but knew it, almost all men in their degree, some time or other, cherish very nearly the same feelings towards the ocean with me." (Herman Melville, novel)

Avoid what we call Multiple POV Disorder, a condition in which the POV is spread everywhere, even to the dog. Authors with this condition should understand that if their story is to unfold in Third Person Omniscient, it

> "Nothing is as important as a likable character. Nothing holds a story together better."
>
> —Ethan Canin

must be established *at the beginning* (see any work by Conrad, Flaubert, Tolstoy). It's our experience that any story is stronger from a single POV; and although it is difficult to write an entire novel in the same POV, it's a certainty that many of the classic novels we remember vividly were written in a single POV—First Person (e.g. *A Catcher in the Rye, Huckleberry Finn)*, or Third Person Subjective (*Great Expectations*). Authors who use multiple POVs—forcing the reader to jump back and forth between perspectives—generally do so to reveal more exposition, but is it worth the risk of losing the authority (and the mystery) of that single *voice*? Explore alternate methods of including exposition without sacrificing the intimacy of that single POV. POV 'jumping' jars the reader and on an unconscious—or even conscious level—removes him or her from the story. Or worse, it breaks the trust the reader had begun to extend to the writer to guide him or her through the narrative.

If, however, the writer is convinced that the story will work only with multiple POVs—Third Person Omniscient—then those voices should be made *distinct* by varying syntax and creating verbal patterns for each character. To be fully involved in the story, the reader should know *at all times* with which character he or she is engaged without the author having to indicate a POV change using signposts (e.g. headings, continually stating the characters' names).

One of the more challenging and interesting voices is the *unreliable narrator*. Written in First Person, this *voice* belongs to someone whose story becomes suspect—is what they're saying true; or is the narrator lying, deluded, or insane (e.g. Gogol's *Diary of a Madman*)? Keeping the reader off-balance with a story that might or might not be true requires dexterity—and an ability to juggle a number of 'fake' storylines at the same time, while keeping the 'true' storyline in play.

Who are these voices?

i)   Often a *voice* (which might contain a strong opening line) will jump out from a newspaper or magazine, or from a conversation overheard on the street, in a café, or on public transit.

ii)   If the writer is sitting quietly, listening, a voice will often materialize, generated by a sensory fragment of someone they've known or met briefly, an individual overheard in public, or someone from a media source. Almost always, the writer's fictional voice is an unconscious reconstruction of someone lodged in their memory.

> "The moment comes when a character does or says something you hadn't thought about. At that moment, he's alive and you leave it to him."
> —Graham Greene

iii) Once you have a fragment, allow others to join in, incident by incident, while letting the voice (character) lead the narrative forward.

iv)   Try contrasting *settings* and *voices*—rework a clichéd character (e.g. a Parisian lover / a car factory employee / friend from Alberta) so the voice seems less common (e.g. a Newfoundland lover / bungee-jump-apparatus factory employee / friend from Tibet), which will allow you to explore new sources of incidents.

v)   What does the tone of *voice* tell us? Is it vulnerable? Deceitful? In pain? Bitter? What connects the reader to the voice telling the story?

- Does the First Person *voice* have an accent or other character traits, as for example a stutter, repetitive words and phrases such as 'cool', 'you know?', 'for that matter', or 'that's awesome'? Does it compulsively lie, exaggerate, over-dramatize, etc.? Does it have a dialect? If so, it might be difficult to sustain and difficult to read.
- In the case of multiple POVs, a verbal tic in the character's thoughts or dialogue indicates immediately to the reader who is speaking.
- With an 'unreliable narrator', you need to ask: Are the lies consistent, believable? And how does one alert the reader to the possibility that the storyteller might not be telling the whole truth?
- Now the voice can be placed in a *setting*.

Setting – Where's The Action?

Patrick Süskind's *Perfume: The Story of a Murderer* sets out the pervasive atmosphere of the novel's setting in the second paragraph:

> "In the period of which we speak, there reigned in the cities a stench barely conceivable to us modern men and women. The streets stank of manure, the courtyards of urine, the stairwells stank of moldering wood and rat droppings, the kitchens spoiled cabbage and mutton fat; the unaired parlours stank of stale dust, the bedrooms of greasy sheets, damp featherbeds, and the pungently sweet aroma of chamber pots. The stench of sulphur rose from the chimneys, the stench of caustic lyes from the tanneries, and from the slaughterhouses came the stench of congealed blood. People stank of sweat and unwashed clothes; from their mouths came the stench of rotting teeth, from

their bellies that of onions, and from their bodies, if they were no longer very young, came the stench of rancid cheese and sour milk and tumorous disease."

"You don't write about the horrors of war. No. You write about a kid's burnt socks lying in the road."

—Richard Price

An effective setting is much more than the description of scenery—it's a primary character. It's the Sahara, the Eiger, the upper Amazon, a blacking-shop in Victorian London, the Arc de Triomphe, the harbour in Algiers or Havana, Hampton Court, Turbaco in Columbia, the shores of Gallipoli, a beach in Australia, your kitchen, or thousands of other locales. In an infinite variety of climatic conditions (rain, snow, fog, heat, etc.), *setting* is the all-pervasive atmosphere holding sway over the characters physically, emotionally, or psychologically.

In any great novel, short story, or biography, *setting* is the surrounding aura within which the protagonist overcomes her or his dilemma (or not). *Setting* influences both narrative and character, and the story's resolution is often contingent (even tangentially) on the protagonist being able to assert him or herself within the setting. *Setting* (like character) can be created with a few specific, animate details. As author Stephen King suggests: "Description begins in the writer's imagination, but should finish in the reader's."

Setting is often a universal presence that threatens to overwhelm the characters and narrative. In Nevil Shute's *On the Beach*, the characters wait in sunny Southern Australia for a cloud of lethal nuclear radiation, the result of an atomic war, to reach them. In *Nineteen Eighty-Four*, Orwell creates a world completely remade into three dictatorships, and the few details in the second paragraph ("smelt of boiled cabbage and old rag mats") place the reader immediately in the day-to-day reality of living in the dank, grim, grey landscape of a totalitarian society, glimpsed in that terrifying "enormous face":

> "The hallway smelt of boiled cabbage and old rag mats. At one end of it a colour poster, too large for indoor display, had been tacked to the wall. It depicted simply an enormous face, more than a metre wide: the face of a man about forty-five, with a heavy black moustache and ruggedly handsome features. Winston made for the stairs. It was no use trying the lift. Even at the best of times it was seldom working, and at present the electric current was cut off during daylight hours. It was part of the economy drive in preparation for Hate Week. The flat was seven flights up, and Winston, who was thirty-nine and had a varicose ulcer above his right ankle, went slowly, resting several times on the way. On each landing, opposite the lift shaft, the poster with the enormous face gazed from the wall. It was one of those pictures which are so contrived that the eyes follow you about when you move. BIG BROTHER IS WATCHING YOU, the caption beneath it ran."

> "Don't use words too big for the subject. Don't say 'infinitely' when you mean 'very'; otherwise you'll have no word left when you want to talk about something really infinite."
> —C.S. Lewis

Both Süskind and Orwell set out worlds of oppression and despair—one setting evoked by smell, the other by smell and sight—immersing the reader in an atmosphere of physical and psychological decay. By the time their protagonists appear, the reader is already part of their coming struggle.

Other settings that cradle the narrative:

Sentimental Education – "On the 15th of September, 1840, at six o'clock in the morning, the *Ville-de-Montereau* was lying alongside the Quai Saint-Bernard, ready to sail, with clouds of smoke pouring from its funnel. People came hurrying up, out of breath; barrels, ropes and baskets of washing lay about in everybody's way; the sailors ignored all inquiries; people bumped into one another; the pile of baggage between the two paddle-wheels grew higher and higher; and the din merged into the hissing of the steam, which, escaping through some iron plates, wrapped the whole scene in a whitish mist, while the bell in the bows went on clanging incessantly." (novel, Gustave Flaubert)

Brideshead Revisited – "Oxford, in those days, was still a city of aquatint. In her spacious and quiet streets men walked and spoke as they had done in Newman's day; her autumnal mists, her grey springtime, and the rare glory of her summer days—such as that day—when the chestnut was in flower and the bells rang out high and clear over her gables and cupolas, exhaled the soft airs of centuries of youth." (novel, Evelyn Waugh)

Dead Souls – "The room was of the familiar sort, for the inn too was of the familiar sort, that is to say, the sort of inn that is to be found in all provincial towns where for a couple of roubles a day travellers are given a quiet room with cockroaches peering out from every corner like prunes, and with a doorway always blocked up by a chest of drawers leading into the next room occupied by a quiet, taciturn, but extremely inquisitive man, who is interested in finding out all the facts about a new arrival." (novel, Nikolai Gogol)

Lady Chatterley's Lover – "Wragby... stood on an eminence in a rather fine old park of oak trees, but alas, one could see in the near distance the chimney of Tevershall pit, with its clouds of steam and smoke, and on the damp, hazy distance of the hill the raw straggle of Tevershall village, a village which began almost at the park gates and trailed in utter hopeless ugliness for a long and gruesome mile: houses, rows of wretched, small, begrimed, brick houses, with black slate roofs for lids, sharp angles and wilful, blank dreariness." (novel, D.H. Lawrence)

The Ginger Man – "Outside, standing in front of the cinema waiting for the roaring tram. It's so noisy, coming down the hill out of the night, mad teetering vehicle. Seems to work like a coffee grinder. But I love the color and the seats, all green and warm, orange, pink and passionate. Like to run up the spiral stairs to the top and see the school-children sitting on the outside platform. I like it because I can see into all the gardens and some of the evening windows. I was impressed by trams when I first set foot in this country. From the top deck you can see into some personal windows. Women wearing slips only. I often saw a great deal of chromium plate in the bedrooms and electric fires glaring from the walls. Also the beds were covered with satin eiderdowns, big, thick and puce." (novel, J.P. Donleavy)

Bouvard and Pécuchet – "Then the horses slowed down, which led to arguments with the driver and the carter. They chose execrable inns, and though they answered for everything, Pécuchet with excessive caution shared their sleeping quarters. The following day they set off at dawn; and the road, endlessly the same, stretched out uphill to the edge of the horizon. The stones continued yard after yard, the ditches were full of water. The countryside spread out in great expanses of cold, monotonous green, clouds chased across the sky, from time to time the rain fell. On the third day squalls blew up. The canvas cover of the wagon was badly fixed and flapped in the wind like the sail of a ship. Pécuchet bowed his head under his cap, and every time he opened his snuff-box had to turn completely round to protect his eyes." (novel, Gustave Flaubert)

> "Writing is not observation— it is feeling."
>
> —Paul Scott

At the beginning of *Jane Eyre*, a vulnerable young woman (Jane) survives a loveless and stark upbringing in the materially and emotionally sparse setting of an orphanage—her emergence into the outside world entirely dependent on her ability to fortify herself against forces larger than her understanding. Enshrouded in the mystery of Thornfield Hall, she is impressed (and unsettled) by its size, and its many rooms, from one of which she hears a "distinct, formal, mirthless" laugh.

In *The Loved One*, after a poke at the British Diaspora in Hollywood of the late 1940s, Evelyn Waugh's description of the expansive and extravagantly landscaped grounds of two types of funeral homes, one for humans ("Whispering Glades")—and one for pets ("The Happier Hunting Ground")—leads the reader into the America of unintentional satire.

"No human being ever spoke of scenery for above two minutes at a time, which makes me suspect that we hear too much of it in literature."

—Robert Louis Stevenson

In *Catch-22*, Joseph Heller's bleakly funny and absurd WWII novel, American Air Force personnel, huddled in tents on a beautiful but desolate Italian island, desperately try to avoid being killed by the senseless determination of the U.S. military to adhere to feckless bureaucratic rules.

In pre-technological eras—pre-World War I—voluminous novels, in which the reader could take up residence, were the norm, and *setting* played a dominant role in establishing their narrative boundaries. Before the advent of radio and television, reading was an active pastime for Victorians who were keenly interested in the physical and cultural landscapes against which the stories were placed. A weighty novel like *Middlemarch: A Study of Provincial Life,* explored life in an English town pre-1832, illustrating how its inhabitants, outside current thought and 'progressive' social attitudes, responded to the multiplicative class mores of the time. For Victorian novelists there were few competing distractions—words being the pre-dominant method of creating pictures in the recipient's mind. Readers with time and income could indulge their passion endlessly; and writers like Trollope, Tolstoy, Gaskell, Flaubert, Balzac, Hugo, Dickens (who went 'viral' in his day), and Thackeray, thought nothing of spending pages describing characters and settings—the countryside, the manor house, the city streets, the factory or the battlefield. Without their stories, we would have little reference to the physical reality of those times.

By the beginning of the twentieth century, the thick effusive novel lost ground to the advance of technology—the telegraph (Morse code) condensing thought to pennies per word; Marconi's talking boxes transmitting the human voice through the air; and, finally, 'moving pictures', the beginning of our obsession with screens. By the 1920s, Hemingway, Fitzgerald, and others had begun retooling the novel, leaving out excessive description—scenery, weather, locale, wardrobe, and character—relying on simple action and dialogue to tell their stories. Throughout the latter half of the twentieth century, setting has been supplanted by technology (in all its various forms: TV, computers, the internet, video games, cell phones, iPods & Pads, etc.), its screens cluttering our minds with hundreds of thousands of images.

"If prose is to be as well written as poetry—the old modernist hope—novelists and readers must develop their own third ears. We have to read musically, testing the precision and rhythm of a sentence, listening for the almost inaudible rustle of historical association clinging to the hems of modern words, attending to patterns, repetitions, echoes, deciding why one metaphor is successful and another is not, judging how the perfect placement of the right verb or adjective seals a sentence with mathematical finality. We must proceed on the assumption that almost all prose popularly acclaimed as beautiful ("she writes like an angel") is nothing of the sort, that almost every novelist will at some point be baselessly acclaimed for writing "beautifully" as almost all flowers are at some point acclaimed for smelling nice."

—James Wood,
How Fiction Works

No longer needing to describe *the where* in voluminous detail, the writer can now establish setting with a few deft strokes.

Theoretically, prose should be shorter and in many cases it is, but recently some writers have produced lengthy novels that incorporate the change described above. *Wolf Hall* by Hilary Mantel is a modern, lengthy, historical novel that doesn't bother with endless setting and character description, its compelling story relying on character and narrative. Based on the life of Thomas More, in the court of Henry VIII, Mantel keeps the action moving, describing very little scenery during the course of its six-hundred-odd pages. Revealing detail is peppered in, but the writing is spare, and the reader never feels that the author has stopped the story to describe the landscape or weather. And yet, because Ms. Mantel's third person subjective *voice* is so rooted in Cromwell's thoughts, the reader is carried raptly through the story of England's eminent Tudor Chancellor.

Setting the Story

i)   In compelling prose, the correlations between setting, voice, and theme (who is telling the story, what is it about and from where is it being told?) are tight. The writer seeks a setting that supports the story's theme or lets the setting suggest a theme (e.g. the destructive power of Alberta's tar sands). A story about the dilatory dangers of wealth, for example, could start in a luxurious mansion, the protagonist a billionaire who, weary of being held captive by his lifestyle (limo, mansion, servants, etc.), ventures into a ghetto on foot to experience the ordinary poor—only to be injured by an SUV driven by a whacked-out drug dealer, who then attempts to kill the billionaire to avoid arrest. Abrupt changes of setting can, in effect, suddenly endanger the protagonist.

ii) Settings that cause friction for the protagonist can create conflict beyond a single individual—what would be the reaction of a Canadian fisherman taking a vacation in the Gulf of Mexico when the BP oil spill occurs? How does the setting alter him, and how does he attempt to affect the setting?

iii) Placing characters (and story) in unusual places (e.g. lovers meet while hanging off the top of the CN Tower) can often help define character.

iv) Throughout the narrative, the reader needs help to visualize where the characters are standing, sitting, lounging, or leaning. What do the characters notice or not notice about the setting? And how do their body language, posture, and mannerisms reveal subtext within the setting?

v) What emotion does the *setting* evoke—joy, oppression, awe, fear—and why. And how does that affect the characters and the narrative?

vi) Lengthy description of scenery or wardrobe stalls the read unless it informs immediately on the narrative. Gore Vidal once reviewed a John Updike novel, pointing out that a lengthy, detailed paragraph describing the intricate craftsmanship of a staircase that Updike's protagonist was ascending did nothing to push his narrative forward.

vii) Setting can be political (the 1930s Depression), forcing the protagonist to struggle against natural or man-made catastrophes, effectively engulfing him or her (and the reader) in despair (e.g. Steinbeck's *The Grapes of Wrath*).

viii) Setting can be mysterious, causing confusion or fear for both reader and protagonist (e.g. O'Brien's *The Third Policeman*).

ix) Setting can, and should, be revealed as the protagonist and peripheral characters move through it. It might contain the obstacles they face, as well as reflect their attributes and flaws, all of which will add to their *characters.*

Characters — Who Are They?

A director of TV commercials, when asked for his opinion of a cameraman with whom he had just worked, remarked, "His pants are too short." This surprised the questioner who, upon reflection, realized that the comment *was* pertinent—*if* the cameraman was less than meticulous about his apparel, was it also true of his work? As a specific, revealing detail in a story, 'pants too short' would immediately bring a character to life for the reader who might remember various pant-leg-challenged individuals in her or his past.

Characters often begin as faint images in the author's mind, conjured up by a word, a phrase, an image, or an action. Usually, writers have only the vaguest idea of who will people the book, but understand that if the characters are allowed to pursue their obsessions, they will soon reveal their personalities. This approach, because of its spontaneity, creates

> "I don't think characters turn out the way you think they are going to turn out. They don't always go your way. At least they don't go my way. If I wanted to start writing about you, by page ten I probably wouldn't be. I don't think you start with a person. I think you start with the parts of many people. Drama has to do with conflict in people, with denials."
>
> —Lillian Hellman,
> *The Paris Review*

narratives flowing from happenstance—incidents generated by characters (resembling those in real life) who are, therefore, more enthralling to the reader. As Evelyn Waugh once explained in a BBC interview:

> "As for the major characters, I really have very little control over them. I start them off with certain preconceived notions... but I constantly find them moving another way. For example, there was the heroine of *Put Out More Flags*, a Mrs. Lyne. I had no idea until halfway through the book that she drank secretly. I could not understand why she behaved so oddly. Then when she sat down on the steps of the cinema I understood all and I had to go back and introduce a series of empty bottles into her flat."

Formed in this way, the characters will do the writing—they will stumble into the obstacles that will plague them. The writer has only to sit and listen, ask questions, and make connections, focusing on those incidents that create the most conflict. By putting the characters in contention with each other the writer creates tension, friction, and finally life itself.

In much prose (fiction and non-fiction), writers often paint their characters in broad strokes to create definable 'good and bad guys'; but realistically-drawn characters—the ones living in your subconscious, having *both* negative and positive qualities—are more interesting to read about. This is often difficult to achieve, because of the subtleties involved, but these 'real' characters are usually enigmatic and captivating to the reader who empathizes with them. We root for and care about people who endure trials and tribulations, and have little or no sympathy for characters who are unaffected by the slings and arrows of outrageous fortune.

We don't need to 'like' a character to be intrigued by him or her (e.g. "Richard III")—we only need to understand his or her motivation. 'Likeable' doesn't necessarily translate into 'riveting', but being driven by inner demons— we all have them—does. Obnoxious characters (e.g. Malvolio in *Twelfth Night*) hold our scrutiny because we recognize their frailty, their tragic flaws. The more intimate the writing, the more universal the story, because each of us suffers from the same hopes, fears, anxieties, and doubts.

> "Front-rank characters should have some defect, some conflicting inner polarity, some real or imagined inadequacy."
> —Barnaby Conrad

Monsieur Charles-Denis-Bartholomé Bovary – "But as he knew no more about farming than he did about calico, as he rode his horses instead of sending them to plough, drank his cider by the bottle instead of selling it by the barrel, ate the finest poultry in his yard and greased his hunting boots with the lard from his pigs, he soon perceived that he had better give up all idea of making money." (*Madame Bovary* – Gustave Flaubert)

Hungry Joe – "...was a jumpy, emaciated wretch with a fleshless face of dingy skin and bone and twitching veins squirming subcutaneously in the blackened hollows behind his eyes like severed sections of snake. It was a desolate, cratered face, sooty with care like an abandoned mining town." (*Catch 22* – Joseph Heller)

> "To Guildenstern and Rosencrantz, Hamlet was a minor player."
> —Henry Miller

Sam Weller – "…habited in a coarse-striped waistcoat, with black calico sleeves, and blue glass buttons; drab breeches and leggings." (*The Pickwick Papers* – Charles Dickens)

Don Quixote – "… there lived a gentleman—one of those who have always a lance in the rack, an ancient shield, a lean hack and a greyhound for coursing. His habitual diet consisted of a stew, more beef than mutton, of hash most nights, boiled bones on Saturdays, lentils on Fridays, and a young pigeon as a Sunday treat; and on this he spent three quarters of his income." (*Don Quixote* – Miguel de Cervantes)

> "You put a character out there and you're in their power. You're in trouble if they're in yours."
>
> —Ann Beattie

Mrs. Wapshot – "…a woman of forty whose fine skin and clear features could be counted among her organizational gifts." (*The Wapshot Chronicle* – John Cheever)

Rollo Martins – "One never knows when the blow may fall. When I saw Rollo Martins first I made this note on him for my security police files: 'In normal circumstances a cheerful fool. Drinks too much and may cause a little trouble. Whenever a woman passes raises his eyes and makes some comment, but I get the impression that really he'd rather not be bothered. Has never really grown up and perhaps that accounts for the way he worshipped Lime.' I wrote there that phrase 'in normal circumstances' because I met him first at Harry Lime's funeral." (*The Third Man*, novella, Graham Greene)

> "The first hundred pages are very tricky, the first forty pages especially. You have to make sure you have the characters you want. That's really the most complicated part."
>
> —Joan Didion, *The Paris Review*

Sancho Panza – "…a neighbour of his [Quixote's] and an honest man—if poor may be called honest—but without much salt in his brain pan." (*Don Quixote* – Miguel de Cervantes)

The General – "José Palacios, his oldest servant, found him floating naked with his eyes open in the purifying waters of his bath and thought he had drowned. He knew this was one of the many ways the General meditated, but the ecstasy in which he lay drifting seemed that of a man no longer of this world. He did not dare come closer but called to him in a hushed voice, complying with the order to awaken him before five so they could leave at dawn. The General came out of his trance and saw in the half-light the clear blue eyes, the curly squirrel-colored hair, the impassive dignity of the steward who attended him every day and who held in his hand a cup of the curative infusion of poppies and gum Arabic. The General's hands lacked strength but he rose up from the medicinal waters in a dolphin-like rush that was surprising in so wasted a body.

'Let's go,' he said, 'as fast as we can. No one loves us here.'" —Gabriel García Márquez, *The General in his Labyrinth*

In his comic novels, Peter De Vries infused his central characters with an unconscious (sometimes conscious) sense of their own irony, as for example in *Reuben Reuben*. Frank Spofford, the first of three protagonists, tells the reader of his life as a chicken farmer, explaining how he came to write it down. Note the strength of that first person voice:

> "Surely the artist must entertain. And one's in a very bad way indeed if one can't laugh. Laughter relaxes the characters in a novel. And if you can make the reader laugh he is apt to get careless and go on reading. So you as the writer get a chance to get something on him."
>
> —Henry Green, *The Paris Review*

Spofford – "I never enrolled in nothing again except for an evening class in creative writing, also in Bridgeport, some years back. I wrote a theme for the class describing my father: 'My father was a rangy man with a long face and the brightest blue eyes you ever see, so it was a shame they were not better lined up than they were, for in that department he resembled Ben Turpin. One eye was always gazing at the other in wrapped admiration. That and wiry hair that stood up straight, like a fright wig, give him a look like one of them drawings that are done by disturbed children in your better schools, that are suppose to show conflict.'" —Peter De Vries, *Reuben, Reuben*

Sometimes an outburst from a character will encapsulate the entire sense of who she or he is:

> Sancho Panza – "'I don't understand that,' said Sancho. 'I only know that while I sleep I have no fear, nor hope, nor trouble, nor glory. God bless the inventor of sleep, the cloak that covers all man's thoughts, the food that cures all hunger, the water that quenches all thirst, the fire that warms the cold, the cold that cools heat; the common coin, in short, that can purchase all things, the balancing weight that levels the shepherd with the king and the simple with the wise. There's only one bad thing about sleep, as I have heard say, and that is that it looks like death; for there's but little difference between a sleeping man and a dead one.'" —Miguel de Cervantes, *Don Quixote*

> "I start with a tingle, a kind of feeling of the story I will write. Then come the characters, and they take over, they make the story."
>
> —Isak Dinesen,
> *The Paris Review*

How do you bring a character to 'life'? Character is revealed through vulnerability, their hopes and fears, behaviours, mannerisms, reactions to events, responses to conflict, incidence and specific, animate detail.

To create narrative, show what happens to the characters—as opposed to telling. *Telling* the reader the character beats his wife will not convince—*showing* the character banging her head against the wall will.

> "A proper noun is something very important in a novel. It is capital. One can no more change a character's name than his skin."
>
> —Gustave Flaubert

Occasionally, *telling* can work if the writer feels the scene isn't driving the story forward; if there's a need to summarize; or if the telling adds complexity to the *voice* (e.g. if the narrator is obviously lying).

Enabling the Characters to Breathe

i) Look for specific, animate detail: clothes (designer-cut, frayed, pants too short, etc.); shelter (monster house, trailer park, spotless, rat-infested, stinks of cabbage / garlic / Lysol, etc.); body (sharp chin, thin hands, legs like sticks, etc.); habits (blinking, sighing, twitching, throat clearing, etc.); speech patterns (repetitive, halting, clichéd, overuse of certain words or phrases: "obviously," "absolutely," "what I'm saying is," "brilliant," etc.)

ii) Show how other characters behave towards the protagonist / antagonist— and how *they* behave towards others. To create a well-rounded character, the reader should know what they do to earn a living, what preoccupies them daily (irritable boss, etc.), with other pertinent psychological detail (parents died young, etc.)

> "Don't say the old lady screamed—bring her on and let her scream."
> —Mark Twain

iii) Nervous habits show us something about the character's emotional state: hair twirling, fingernail biting, hands clasping, forced smiling, insincere or nervous laughing. Revelation of the character is also possible through monologue (stream-of-consciousness) or dialogue, but the narrative must keep chugging on.

iv) Exposition overload will overwhelm and stall the read. Only a few specific, animate details are required; the reader will flesh out the complexities of the character in his or her imagination. Less is more. Keep us guessing; don't over-explain—the most compelling characters have mystery.

v)   The intrepid writer spends time loitering in public places, observing and listening to the conversations and fragments of conversations of *real* people (also a possible source of themes, incidents, and dialogue). Jon De Vries observed that when his father, the comic novelist Peter De Vries, was to be found standing in the streets of his home town of Westport, Connecticut wearing a blank expression, he was eavesdropping on the conversations around him in the streets and shops. Writers tend to be acutely attentive to what people wear, do, and say, and how they respond to others. Often major characters emerge from the slightest of details.

> "A good novel tells us the truth about its hero; but a bad novel tells us the truth about its author."
>
> —G.K. Chesterton

vi)   Be aware of characters becoming too self-absorbed. Self-devoted characters—unless created for comedic effect (e.g. Molière's *The Imaginary Invalid*)—are not likely to be vulnerable, raising no curiosity in the reader, who loses empathy with them (e.g. our 'blog' culture often leans to endless self-examination, verging on the narcissistic).

vii)   Characters should be left unprotected, exposed, vulnerable. Make them take their gloves off and go at it.

> "I give them [her characters] their heads. They furnish their own nooses."
>
> —Dawn Powell

viii)   Love all your characters, good, bad, and indifferent. No matter what they get up to, empathize with their plight. It's not enough to reveal their dark side, show why it exists (e.g. often Dickens features a child who has been orphaned or forced to live in a debtors' prison). Make the reader care enough to want to keep reading.

ix) Find the humour inherent in character situations—humour is our defence against the vagaries of life. There is a difference between laughing with your characters, and laughing at them. Laughing at is mockery, and indicates a lack of compassion for the character. In laughing with the reader identifies (and empathizes) with the character's dilemma.

x) If the writer's in sync with his or her characters, when they open their mouths, they will speak lively and credible *dialogue*.

Dialogue – Are You Talking to Me?

Many will recognize the line above from the movie TAXI DRIVER. Alone in his room, Travis, the lonely, alienated cabbie, dressed as a guerrilla fighter (his scalp sprouting a Mohawk), admires his reflection in the mirror as he practices drawing a gun, threatening imagined adversaries with different readings of the line: "are you talking to *me*?"… "I said, *are* you talking to me?" This abrupt change in him shows us a previously-hidden aspect of Travis' personality, and immediately signals danger; he's clearly unbalanced and angry; and it makes us uneasy.

From the information available, it appears that the scene was improvised by the actor, Robert De Niro. It's likely that, had the scene been written as presented before shooting, its purpose would not have been understood, and calls would have been made for it to be rewritten.

In all prose, *dialogue* can be a useful tool in driving the narrative on, disclosing the time

> "Dialogue has to show not only something about the speaker that is its own revelation, but also maybe something about the speaker he doesn't know but the other character does know."
>
> —Eudora Welty

and place in which the story occurs, reinforcing the author's theme, and occasionally unsettling the reader:

Sam Weller, *The Pickwick Papers* – 'I lodged in the same house vith a pieman once, sir, and wery nice man he was—reg'lar clever chap, too—make pies of o' anything, he could. "What a number o' cats you keep, Mr. Brooks," says I, when I'd got intimate vith him. "Ah," says he, "I do—a good many," says he. "You must be wery fond o' cats," says I. "Other people is," says he, a winkin' at me; "they an't in season till the winter though," says he. "Not in season!" says I. "No," says he, "fruits is in, cats is out." "Why, what do you mean?" says I. "Mean?" says he. "That I'll never be a party to the combination o' the butchers, to keep up the prices o' meat," says he. "Mr. Weller," says he, a squeezing my hand wery hard, and vispering in my ear—"don't mention this here agin—but it's the seasonin' as does it. They're all made o' them noble animals," say he, a pointin' to a wery nice little tabby kitten, "and I seasons 'em for beefsteak, weal, or kidney, 'cordin to the demand. And more than that," says he, "I can make a weal a beefsteak, or a beefsteak a kidney, or any one on 'em a mutton, at a minute's notice, just as the market changes, and appetites wary!"'—Charles Dickens

Major Sanderson and Yossarian, *Catch-22* – "Major Sanderson flew instantly into a rage. 'Can't you even do one thing right?' he pleaded, turning beet-red with vexation and crashing the sides of both fists down upon his desk together. 'The trouble with you is that you think you're too good for all the conventions of society. You probably think you're too good for me too, just because I arrived at puberty late. Well, do you know what you are? You're a frustrated, unhappy, disillusioned, undisciplined, maladjusted young man!' Major Sanderson's disposition seemed to mellow as he reeled off the uncomplimentary adjectives.

'Yes, sir,' Yossarian agreed carefully. 'I guess you're right.'

'Of course, I'm right. You're immature. You've been unable to adjust to the idea of war.'

'Yes, sir.'

'You have a morbid aversion to dying. You probably resent the fact that you're at war and might get your head blown off any second.'

'I more than resent it, sir. I'm absolutely incensed.'

"You have deep-seated survival anxieties. And you don't like bigots, bullies, snobs or hypocrites. Subconsciously there are many people you hate."

'Consciously, sir, consciously,' Yossarian corrected in an effort to help. 'I hate them consciously.'

'You're antagonistic to the idea of being robbed, exploited, degraded, humiliated or deceived. Misery depresses you. Ignorance depresses you. Persecution depresses you. Violence depresses you. Slums depress you. Greed depresses you. Crime depresses you. Corruption depresses you. You know, it wouldn't surprise me if you're a manic-depressive!'" (Joseph Heller)

The Man with no name and Sergeant Pluck, *The Third Policeman* – "'I was once acquainted with a tall man,' he said to me at last, 'that had no name either and you are certain to be his son and the heir to his nullity and all his nothings. What way is your pop today and where is he?'

It was not, I thought, entirely reasonable that the son of a man who had no name should have no name also but it was clear that the Sergeant was confusing me with somebody else. This was no harm and I decided to encourage him. I considered it desirable that he should know nothing about me but it was even better if he knew several things which were quite wrong. It would help me in using him for my own purposes and ultimately in finding the black box.

'He is gone to America,' I replied.

'Is that where,' said the Sergeant. 'Do you tell me that? He was a true family husband. The last time I interviewed him it was about a missing pump and he had a wife and ten sonnies and at that time he had the wife again in a very advanced state of sexuality.'

'That was me,' I said smiling.

'That was you,' he agreed. "What way are the ten strong sons?"
'All gone to America.'
'That is a great conundrum of a country,' said the Sergeant, 'a very wide territory, a place occupied by black men and strangers. I am told they are very fond of shooting-matches in that quarter.'
'It is a queer land,' I said." (Flann O'Brien)

Letting the Characters Speak

i)   By excluding the clutter and repetitions of 'street speech', *written* dialogue allows the narrative to flow.

ii) The reader's interest is immediately caught when dialogue shows conflict between the characters.

iii) When we speak, we're often in motion (walking, getting up or down, running, cooking, eating, twitching, working, selling, buying, etc.), presenting different aspects of our characters. Accompanied by gesture or action, dialogue can reveal subtext ('"How do you mean I'm insincere?" he asked abruptly, tapping his fingers on the table.')

iv) How often do we say what we mean? Subtext is continually running through our thoughts—what we really *want* to say. Does the character mean what she or he says? Or does dialogue expose him or her as duplicitous? If so, in what ways? How do you show a character expressing "terminological inexactitude" (Churchill's eloquent euphemism for 'lying')? Does she avert her eyes? Speak forcefully? Smile too much?

v)   When bringing two characters together, don't slow the narrative with pleasantries (i.e. "Hello," "how are you?," etc.) unless the subtext warrants it (e.g. the characters despise each other but are being disingenuous for ulterior motives). Skip the introductions and goodbyes. Come into the scene late and leave early.

vi)   If the dialogue is sparse, it will add mystery to the characters (shades of Harold Pinter), and the narrative will flow much quicker.

vii)   Adverbs should be employed sparingly. The use of one in dialogue (e.g. a character who uses the word "totally" as an affirmative) can help to define a character, or show contradiction (e.g. "I love you," he said bitterly.) but their overuse slows the narrative.

viii)   To access 'real' dialogue, sit in the midst of a restaurant or crowded public area, and note the bits of conversation you hear. Write down the talk of people around you, the words they use, the phrases they repeat, their speech rhythms, then match their style and write your version of what comes next. "'Xcuse me,' the fatter one says, pulling apart an apple fritter, 'but that's not what she told me.' I says, 'someone's lying around here, and it don't make me feel good… 'Xcuse me,' I says, 'that's very nice, but do you love me?'" (Cordelia Strube, *Teaching Pigs to Sing*)

> "When I was writing *The Shadow of the Glen*, some years ago, I got more aid than any learning could have given me from a chink in the floor of the old Wicklow house where I was staying, that let me hear what was being said by the servant girls in the kitchen."
> —John Millington Synge

ix)   Read dialogue aloud. Is it easy to say? Do you stumble over the words, run out of breath? As Bertolt Brecht noted, "Simplicity is so very difficult."

x)   Avoid plugging dialogue with exposition. It's tempting but deadly to slip background information into dialogue. Too much information dulls the reader's curiosity, and real conversations rarely offer much story information. Question your dialogue. Seasoned screenwriters test each line they write with "who asked?" to determine if the exposition is necessary. If the reader can say, "Who asked?" on some unconscious (or conscious) level, the disclosures are too obvious.

xi) Dialogue scenes centred around conflict or misunderstanding push the narrative line forward and offer opportunities for humour or pathos; although on film—not obvious on the page—a scene without dialogue, revealing the character's inner conflicts in his or her facial expressions, can be emotionally forceful.

xii) Matching dialogue to action assists the reader's imagination to place the characters. Suspended dialogue—talk not tied to setting—will distract the reader, causing her to wonder where the characters are standing (sitting, lounging). The use of sparse, specific, animate detail will place the characters in the setting. Once the reader understands *where* the characters are, they will absorb more easily *who* they are—from what they say, how they say it, and their body language and mannerisms as they say it. Accompanying dialogue with action reduces the need to attribute dialogue.

xiii) One of Elmore Leonard's Ten Rules of Writing is: "Never use a verb other than 'said' to carry dialogue." We respectfully disagree with Mr. Leonard. Using only the word 'said' to carry dialogue is, to us, like using the word 'walk' to describe all self-locomotion (i.e. trot, stride, amble, etc.). English is a robust language rich in expressive possibilities, and many incisive verbs exist to convey the tone of the dialogue and the character's mood (e.g. sneered, snorted, whined, mumbled, bellowed, gasped, panted, called, shouted, murmured, etc.), so why use only one? Isn't the reader capable of understanding the meaning of more than one verb? What would Dickens, Austen, *et al* have written?

xiv) The best *dialogue* is simple. In a two-character situation, the dialogue reinforces the conflict / mystery / miscommunication between the characters. In a screenplay, there should be minimal camera direction—the director is paid extremely handsomely to determine what the camera sees. The screenwriter is therefore responsible for ensuring that the dialogue moves the narrative forward smartly; that each scene has conflict and is integral to the story; and that the narrative has an arc—a beginning, middle and an end. Effective dialogue and specific, animate character-description in each scene will assist the actors and director immeasurably.

> "Terrence Rattigan on the main problem of playwriting.
>
> 'It is the implicit, rather than the explicit, that gives life to a scene," he said. The main problem in playwriting, he added, "was what *not* to have your actors say, and how best *not* to have them say it.'"
>
> —From "Vile Bodies" by John Lahr, *The New Yorker*, October 17, 2011

xv) Be aware of characters' speech patterns. Some might have definite rhythms and others no rhythm at all, especially those who tend to ramble. Not all characters need to have a rhythm. Putting a rhythmic-speaking and a non-rhythmic-speaking character together in a scene produces an interesting polarity—adding to the conflict.

In the two screenplay scenes below, note the simplicity of the dialogue, the minimal but effective description of the characters' actions, and the unresolved differences between the two characters, creating the tension. Note how little exposition there is—no description of the restaurant or the other patrons, or what the characters are wearing.

INT – NIGHT – RESTAURANT
JO and ALEX sit at the table, reading menus.

ALEX

So what did you do all week?

JO

Umm... I dunno... not much.

ALEX

Did you party?

JO

Not really.

ALEX

You were out a lot.

JO

I guess.
   (defensively)
I can't list off for you what I did.

ALEX

I'm just trying to make conversation.

JO

I appreciate it, sweetheart ... how was Montreal?

ALEX

Great.

Silence. ALEX glances around the restaurant.

JO

Did you meet some nice people?

ALEX

Yeah...
   (plays with his knife)

JO

Who'd you hang out with?

ALEX

Oh mostly the guys.

JO

Yeah?

ALEX

Yeah, we went dancing, stuff like that ... the bars are open late there.

JO

I know.

ALEX

Other than that I just took it easy. Met a girl I went to school with, that was great.

JO

(looks at him)
Great.
He avoids her eyes, playing with his knife.

JO

(realizing)
Alex... sometimes sleeping with another person... works as a catalyst in understanding where your present relationship is going...

ALEX

I know...
(looks at the floor)

JO

I mean it's not necessarily a bad thing ...

ALEX

Yeah...
They sit absolutely still, she looking at him, he looking at the floor.

JO

Did you sleep with someone?
Jo watches him. He stares at his plate.

ALEX

I really don't want to talk about this here...

(looks around the room)
She watches him play with the stem of his glass.

ALEX

Yes...

(looks at her)

... I thought you'd left... you were never home when I called. I
was jealous. I freaked out.

JO, looking at him, has her fingers tight around her wine glass.

ALEX

I could confess to her. We talked about you all night. She
understood.

JO sips her wine.

ALEX

It was the anonymity of it that attracted me, you know what I
mean?

JO

(not angry)

No.

ALEX

I wish I hadn't done it because it destroyed a friendship.

JO (V.O.)

If I tell you, you'll pull away from me. We'll never get it
straight.

He searches her face for some reaction.

JO covers her mouth with her hand, closes her eyes, trying not to cry.
ALEX reaches under the table, caressing her leg.
She tries to speak to him but can't stop crying. She uses a napkin,
hiding her eyes by bending over her plate to eat.

JO

(gently)

Eat your supper, it'll get cold.

(forces herself to eat)

ALEX

Are you hungry?

JO

No.

She stuffs more food in her mouth. ALEX stops eating, watching her.

ALEX

I didn't want to tell you but you sensed it.

(*sympathetically*)

Do you want more wine?

She nods.

ALEX

(*pouring the wine*)

What are you thinking?

JO

I don't know... I'm confused.

She stops trying to eat. ALEX begins eating again but without enthusiasm.

JO (V.O.)

Sleeping with Steven's no different than Alex's fucking a stranger.

JO

I don't want you to feel guilty. I told you you could if the situation came up... I understand why you did it. I really do. I would have done the same except there wasn't anyone around I wanted to fuck.

JO (V.O.)

Liar.

JO puts her head in her hands, hiding from him.

JO

I'm glad you told me. So don't feel guilty. It was something you had to do.

ALEX

I wouldn't have done it if we weren't fighting all the time.

(*thinks*)

I don't know, maybe it's something men have to do. Ted screws around on Lisa. She lives with it.

JO

Ted makes me sick and Lisa's a wimp.

>   ALEX
>
> You don't even know...
>
>   JO
>
> I'm sorry I don't buy that. Lisa's taking it means nothing to me.
> I'll take it once because I said you could do it but if you ever,
> ever do it again... out.

*She holds back tears of frustration. ALEX watches her. She hides her
face in her hands.*

>   ALEX
>
> I'm saying that it made me realize I don't need to do it.
>
>   JO
>
> Three months ago I said I'd kill you if you screwed some-
> one else. Now I'm sitting here taking it. It says a lot about the
> deterioration of relationships, doesn't it?

*He reaches for her hand, nearly knocking over a glass. JO steadies the
glass, moves it.*

>   ALEX
>
> Give me your hand?
>
>   *(she gives it to him.)*
>
> What you said about it making a person re-evaluate what he
> has. I realized that I have everything. Baby, I can't get by with
> out you...
>
>   *(tries not to cry)*
>
> ... I can't. I value you so much ... I can't... please forgive me?
>
>   JO
>
> Please forgive me.

*She takes his hand and holds it palm forwards against her face, cov-
ering her eyes.*

INT – NIGHT – DANCE CLUB

*On the dance floor, JO and ALEX slow dance, bodies pressed together,
tender, careful of each other, hardly moving. The music is earsplitting,
contradicting their movement. They are in their own world, oblivious
of the flashing lights.*

                                    ALEX
        Is the music too loud?
                                     JO
        Yes.
                                    ALEX
        Do you want to go home?
                                     JO
        Yes.
        He leads her out by the hand.[1]

Syntax – Which Word Where

The order in which you place your words—the ones generating the images you're trying to slip into the reader's mind—is critical. So is the order of the sentences, the ones containing incidents which create character and generate further incidents, evolving into a narrative.

> Prose: "words in their best order."
> —Samuel Coleridge

The following opening is particularly evocative:

The Horse's Mouth – "I was walking by the Thames. Half-past morning on an autumn day. Sun in a mist. Like an orange in a fried fish shop. All bright below. Low tide, dusty water and a crooked bar of straw, chicken-boxes, dirt and oil from mud to mud. Like a viper swimming in skim milk. The old serpent, symbol of nature and love.
Five windows light the caverned man:
Through one he breathes the air;
Through one hears music of the spheres,
Through one can look
And see small portions of the eternal world.

---

1. From the screenplay of "FINE" written by Cordelia Strube and Barry Healey, based on the play "FINE" by Cordelia Strube.

Such as Thames mud turned into a bank of nine carat gold rough from the fire. They say a chap just out of prison runs into the nearest cover; into some dark little room, like a rabbit put up by a stoat. The sky feels too big for him. But I liked it. I swam in it. I couldn't take my eyes off the clouds, the water, the mud. And I must have been hopping up and down Greenbank hard for half an hour grinning like a gargoyle, until the wind began to get up my trousers and down my back, and to bring me to myself, as they say. Meaning my liver and lights.

And I perceived that I hadn't time to waste on pleasure. A man of my age has to get on with the job." (novel, Joyce Cary)

The first three short sentences place the narrator in the setting (walking by the Thames on a sunny Autumn day); the next five, simply and imaginatively, allude to the beauty of the scene (the sun and the riverbank as a painter might see them), leading into the lines by William Blake which suggest the protagonist's philosophy. The next paragraph lets us know that this man is "a chap just out of prison," who doesn't have "time to waste on pleasure" but whose zestful outlook tells us that,

"This is the sort of English up with which I will not put."
—Winston Churchill

"I couldn't take my eyes off the clouds, the water, the mud..." and that he was "...hopping up and down Greenbank hard for half an hour grinning like a gargoyle, until the wind began to get up my trousers and down my back, and to bring me to myself, as they say." These sentences endear the character to the reader; and the final two let the reader know that this man is old and urgently must attend to something. We don't know as yet that he's a painter—although his vivid perspective engages us immediately, and we want to know what he's about to get up to. Those first sentences, in any other order (without the images), would not have worked half so well.

The order of words and phrases in a sentence—and sentences in a paragraph—can accelerate or impede your narrative, having a direct impact on the read. (Note: All the excerpts included in this book contain superb syntax.)

Grammar and spelling are important but, in terms of storytelling, do not carry the same weight as *theme, narrative, voice,* etc. Prose can be grammatically correct and accurately spelled but still fail to hook the reader. A capable editor can often smooth out the grammar and spelling—and might even be able to suggest how to edit the story substantively—but it's unlikely he or she will understand how the order of words and sentences evolved in the mind of the writer.

In movies, where the image is all-important, the emphasis on grammar and spelling is not essential—but, for both books and movies, narrative is paramount and greatly affected by *syntax,* crafted by the order of images and thoughts as encountered by the viewer. In a novel, the writer places the words, phrases, and sentences in an order which heightens the reader's curiosity to maximum effect—tragic or comedic or both. The quote by Philip Roth ironically details the daily preoccupation of

"Cast iron rules will not answer... what is one man's colon is another man's comma."

—Mark Twain

"I turn sentences around. That's my life. I write a sentence and then I turn it around. Then I look at it and I turn it around again. Then I have lunch. Then I come back in and write another sentence. Then I have tea and turn the new sentence around. Then I read the two sentences over and turn them both around. Then I lie down on my sofa and think. Then I get up and throw them out and start from the beginning. And if I knock off from this routine for as long as a day, I'm frantic with boredom and a sense of waste."

—Philip Roth, *The Ghost Writer*

a writer searching endlessly for the most flowing method of revealing his or her story.

Sometimes, the oddest usage trumps the most correct. As an example, note how the first sentence below has less impact than the second because the sequence of events as described in the second resembles, and thereby suggests, the awkwardness of that failed kiss. The first is grammatically more correct but pedantic, while the syntax of the second suggests the confused emotions of the character.

Ed tried to kiss Melanie on the forehead, but she lifted her chin and he missed, smacking his head on her lips.	← less impact than →	Ed smacked his head on Melanie's lips when he tried to kiss her on the forehead as she was lifting her chin.

Working Out the Syntax

i)   Play with the sentences until you find sequences of words and phrases that have their own unique rhythm; that surprise and please; that define the characters, yet pique the reader's curiosity.

ii) Keep the images and ideas simple and clear in the first few paragraphs. Don't overload the reader with too much information or too many characters. Ease into the story.

In the excerpt below, from the first page of Charles Dickens's *Bleak House*, the description at first glance seems ponderous; but Dickens leads the reader into the setting using the word "fog" as a thematic motif. *Voice* (Third Person Omniscient) and *setting* are strongly evoked in the images; the order of which, from the rural country-side, on down the Thames to the docks of London and then leading up to "... the very heart of the fog"... where "... sits the Lord High Chancellor in his High Court of Chancery," signals the real beginning of the novel. The writing is colourful, and one wonders how many times Dickens rewrote those paragraphs. Did he create the syntax, and that distinct rhythm, in his mind before sitting down at his desk? It's difficult to imagine these words and phrases in any other order—note how the repetition of the omnipresent 'fog' (sixteen times), along with specific, animate detail, creates suspense, transporting the reader into Victorian England:

> "The maker of a sentence launches out into the infinite and builds a road into Chaos and old Night, and is followed by those who hear him with something of wild, creative delight."
> —Ralph Waldo Emerson

Bleak House – "Fog everywhere. Fog up the river, where it flows among green aits and meadows; fog down the river, where it rolls defiled among the tiers of shipping, and the waterside pollutions of a great (and dirty) city. Fog on the Essex marshes, fog on the Kentish heights. Fog creeping into the cabooses of collier-brigs; fog lying out on the yards, and hovering in the rigging of great ships; fog drooping on the gunwales of barges and small boats. Fog in the eyes and throats of ancient Greenwich pensioners, wheezing by the firesides of their wards; fog in the stem and bowl of an afternoon pipe of the wrathful skipper, down in his close cabin; fog cruelly pinching the toes and fingers of his shivering little 'prentice boy on deck. Chance people on the bridges peeping over the parapets into a nether sky of fog, with fog all round them, as if they were up in a balloon, and hanging in the misty clouds.

> "The greatest masterpiece in literature is only a dictionary out of order."
> — Jean Cocteau

Gas looming through the fog in divers places in the streets, much as the sun may, from the spongey fields, be seen to loom by husband-man and ploughboy. Most of the shops lighted two hours—as the gas seems to know, for it has a haggard and unwilling look.

The raw afternoon is rawest, and the dense fog is densest, and the muddy streets are muddiest, near that leaden-headed old obstruction, appropriate ornament for the threshold of a leaden-headed old cor-poration: Temple Bar. And hard by Temple Bar in Lincoln's Inn Hall, at the very heart of the fog, sits the Lord High Chancellor in his High Court of Chancery." (novel, Charles Dickens)

Improving Your Syntax

Takes practice. Keep turning your sentences around.

4. Openings – Grab Them by the Gotchees

Here's how the Purchase Test works—walk into any bookstore and pick up a novel. Open it to the first page and begin reading. Does the protagonist immediately engage you? Are you inside the story in seconds? If not, put it down and go on to the next. Repeat the procedure until, eventually, you open a book, a character grabs you by the throat, and yanks you into the narrative. That book, written in succinct prose, will have no clutter—*no lengthy, baffling, overly descriptive prologue in italics*—and the story will absorb you instantly. That's the one you will purchase.

> "How many good books suffer neglect through the inefficiency of their beginnings?"
> —Edgar Allan Poe

To write such a book, you might spend years of toil. As Orwell suggested, "Writing a book is a horrible, exhausting struggle, like a long bout of some painful illness."

To see it published, you raise the odds in your favour by sending a civil, well-researched, and lucid letter to an agent or publisher, explaining why your book is timely and why it's for them. Inquire if they would be amenable to reading your MS. And include the first chapter—but only if it's volatile. Your first sentences are very important; they should excite, enthrall, and intrigue.

> "I always do the first line well, but I have trouble doing the others."
> —Molière,
> *The Ridiculous Précieuses*

Once the agent's or publisher's assistant has received your MS, opened it, and been snared by the narrative, your work might go on to excite the agent and / or the publisher. Yet there is no guarantee even then that your book will see print if it doesn't titillate the marketing department.

Although hype, target marketing, literary awards, and Oprah can move thousands of books, success for a book that's 'unputdownable' (Raymond Chandler) begins with startling prose.

Below are some examples of eminent authors setting snares for the reader. Note how, in the first example, Graham Greene sets up the character *and* the setting in the opening paragraph by raising questions in the reader's mind (i.e. who is Hale, where is he, who wants to murder him and why, and what 'holiday crowd'?):

"All good writing is swimming under water and holding your breath."
—F. Scott Fitzgerald

Brighton Rock – "Hale knew, before he had been in Brighton three hours, that they meant to murder him. With his inky fingers and his bitten nails, his manner cynical and nervous, anybody could tell he didn't belong—belong to the early summer sun, the cool Whitsun wind off the sea, the holiday crowd. They came in by train from Victoria every five minutes, rocked down Queen's Road standing on the tops of the little local trams, stepped off in bewildered multitudes into fresh and glittering air: the new silver paint sparkled on the piers, the cream houses ran away into the west like a pale Victorian water-colour; a race in miniature motors, a band playing, flower gardens in bloom below the front, an aeroplane advertising something for the health in pale vanishing clouds across the sky." (novel, Graham Greene)

The Tin Drum – "Granted: I'm an inmate in a mental institution; my keeper watches me, scarcely lets me out of his sight, for there's a peep-hole in the door, and my keeper's eye is the shade of brown that can't see blue-eyed types like me." (novel, Günter Grass)

The Handyman – "Gerald Muspratt gave no indication of what he was about to do. He walked over to the French windows in the dining room to inspect the weather and, without even turning round, died. After he had done so – while he was doing it – Phyllis ran from the end of the table, a long way to the empty window. The expression on his face was peaceful, his eyes and mouth shut and composed. He had even fallen quite neatly for an elderly man, one hand tucked under his cheek as though he were snoozing. But undeniably dead, gone for ever. At first she trembled with shock, all of a dither; swivelled on her haunches, not knowing which way to turn, panting little gasps which sounded like oh dear, oh dear God, oh; her hands fluttered, patting, pulling at his hairy tweed jacket then flying away as though stung. She saw the table from an unknown angle, the packet of Bran Flakes blocking the ceiling, the heavy arches of the toast-rack tarnished on the inside, the shadow beneath the rim of the plate over which the dead man's mar-malade oozed. What to do? Could he be left alone? She stumbled to her feet, took a few paces, looked back imploring him to stay there, blundered away again; and then, miraculously, the sound of the back door opening and slamming, the crash and puff of Mrs. Rodburn's morning arrival." (novel, Penelope Mortimer)

The Outsider – "Mother died today. Or maybe yesterday. I don't know. I had a telegram from home: 'Mother passed away. Funeral tomorrow. Yours sincerely.' That doesn't mean anything. It may have been yes-terday." (novel, Albert Camus)

A Perfect Day for Bananafish – "There were ninety-seven New York advertising men in the hotel, and, the way they were monopolizing the long-distance lines, the girl in 507 had to wait from noon till almost two-thirty to get her call through. She used the time, though. She read an article in a women's pocket-sized magazine, called 'Sex is Fun – or Hell.' She washed her comb and brush. She took the spot out of the skirt of her beige suit. She moved the button on her Saks blouse. She tweezed out two freshly surfaced hairs in her mole. When the operator finally rang her room, she was sitting on the window seat and had almost finished putting lacquer on the nails of her left hand." (*9 Stories*, J.D. Salinger)

The Heart Fails Without Warning – "September: when she began to lose weight at first, her sister had said, I don't mind; the less of her the better. It was only when Morna grew hair—fine down on her face, in the hollow curve of her back—that Lola began to complain. I draw the line at hair, she said. This is a girls' bedroom, not a dog kennel." (short story, Hilary Mantel)

Notes From Underground – "I am a sick man. ... I am an angry man. I am an unattractive man. I think there is something wrong with my liver. But I don't understand the least thing about my illness, and I don't know for certain what part of me is affected. I am not having any treatment for it, and never have had, although I have a great respect for medicine and for doctors. I am besides extremely superstitious, if only in having such respect for medicine. (I am well educated enough not to be superstitious, but superstitious I am.) No, I refuse treatment out of spite. This is something you will probably not understand. Well, I understand it. I can't of course explain who my spite is directed against in this manner; I know perfectly well that I can't 'score off' the doctors in any way by not consulting them; I know better than anybody that I am harming nobody but myself. All the same, if I don't have treatment, it is out of spite. Is my liver out of order?—let it get worse!" (novella, Fyodor Dostoyevsky).

The Good Soldier Švejk – "'So they've killed Ferdinand,' said the charwoman to Mr. Švejk who, having left the army many years before, when a military medical board had declared him to be chronically feeble-minded, earned a livelihood by the sale of dogs—repulsive mongrel monstrosities for whom he forged pedigrees. Apart from this occupation, he was afflicted with rheumatism, and was just rubbing his knees with embrocation.

"Which Ferdinand, Mrs. Miller?" asked Švejk, continuing to massage his knees. "I know two Ferdinands. One of them does jobs for Prusa the chemist, and one day he drank a bottle of hair oil by mistake; and then there's Ferdinand Kokoska who goes round collecting manure. They wouldn't be any great loss, either of'em."

"No, it's the Archduke Ferdinand, the one from Konopiste, you know, Mr. Švejk, the fat, pious one.'" (novel, Jaroslav Hašek)

Stained Glass – "She thought he was a decent enough man until she tried to break up with him. They were sitting in the back of a restaurant drinking decaffeinated coffee; she was gesturing with her hands and saying that this *thing*, their relationship, wasn't going anywhere and that he knew it. His hands lay flat in his lap as he listened to her, and his blue eyes never moved in his bland pudgy face. When he didn't respond to what she had said, she stood up. He reached out for her arm, missed it, and knocked over his water glass. It was nearly empty, and only the ice cubes spilled out on the tablecloth, sliding in her direction. She looked at him, paid for her half of the bill, and walked out to her Toyota. She was turning the key in the ignition when, hearing something, she looked to her left at the window and saw his hand scrabbling against the glass. She had already pressed down the lock. She heard his voice coming in gasping explosive waves from behind his hand. Only three of his words were audible: '...can't... do... this.' She shifted the Toyota into first gear, released the clutch, and drove out of the parking lot, seeing him, slouched and coiled, receding in the rearview mirror." (short story, Charles Baxter, from *Through the Safety Net*)

> "Whether it's something that happened twenty years ago or only yesterday, I must start out with an emotion—one that's close to me and that I can understand."
>
> —F. Scott Fitzgerald

Grabbing Them by the Gotchees

i)   Our attention is always drawn to actions in the middle of conflicts. By throwing the protagonist up against an obstacle, or placing him or her in an incident, the writer dares the reader to find out 'why'.

ii) Try describing incidents—not the scenery—to move the story forward. Make the reader aware ASAP of what's at stake—*something* must be at stake to pull her or him instantly into the story's emotional centre.

iii) Never complain, never explain. Withhold some information to create questions in the reader's mind—Who is she? Where is he, and why? What are they doing? What are they saying and why? What do they mean? Where are they going?

iv) Omit needless words. Use only essential words to move the narrative forward. Make each one earn its position on the page. First drafts are by necessity overwritten; rewriting consists of purging unnecessary words.

v)   Tightening the opening might generate ideas on how to imagine an *ending.*

5. Endings — the Sense of One

Endings can be the most difficult part of prose. If you're a novelist, and have just spent years of sweat and emotional toil constructing characters, incidents, and a narrative, you might begin to panic as you close in on your ending.

Fear not. Although intimidated by the clever ones who have the last sentence in mind before beginning the first, remember Doctorow ("Writing is like driving at night..."). You've managed to make it this far without losing the reader, and so far the words on the page or screen aren't too embarrassing. So, as you search for a believable resolution, let your mind play.

If your instincts are unfettered, the ending will become apparent, appearing at the last possible moment. All those random thoughts that led to the accumulation of incidents and characters will, after cogitating in your neurons for a time, offer up a persuasive—possibly unpleasant or ambiguous—ending, leaving the reader with new insight into a previously obscured world.

> "Life goes on, and for the sake of verisimilitude and realism, you cannot possibly give the impression of an ending: you must let something hang. A cheap interpretation of that would be to say that you must always leave a chance for a sequel. People die, love dies, but life does not end, and so long as people live, stories must have life at the end."
>
> —John O'Hara

> "If you are going to make a book end badly, it must end badly from the beginning."
>
> —Robert Louis Stevenson

Be wary of endings found at the Happy-Ever-After-School-of-Writing, an institute which instructs the writer to leave his or her world more perfect than she or he found it. A nicely tied-up plot might satisfy some—the ones not wanting to have their values questioned—but for readers seeking a deeper sense of materiality (even catharsis), it won't do.

"Finishing a book is just like you took a child out in the yard and shot it."
—Truman Capote

In the case of 'permanent' (lasting) literature, the author of the memorable novel (biography, etc.) ignores plot, while attempting to build a denser, more candid, and resonant relationship with the reader.

Frank Kermode, in *The Sense of an Ending*, suggests that, "A novel has this (and more) in common with love, that it is, so to speak, delighted with its own inventions of character, but must represent their uniqueness and their freedom... without losing the formal qualities that make it a novel. The truly imaginative novelist has an unshakable 'respect for the contingent'; without it he sinks into fantasy, which is a way of deforming reality. 'Since reality is incomplete, art must not be too afraid of incompleteness,' says Miss [Iris] Murdoch. We must not falsify it with patterns too neat, too inclusive; *there must be dissonance [italics ours]*. 'Literature must always represent a battle between real people and images'."

"My last page is always latent in my first; but the intervening windings of the way become clear only as I write."
—Edith Wharton

Were we to offer examples of great endings, it would be necessary to include the entire work (novel, biography, etc.) to allow the reader to see how the narrative determines the ending, making this work far too large to lift and too expensive to publish; but we can offer the following:

Finding an Ending

i) The narrative can be considered ended when all the characters are exhausted, dead, or removed by circumstances beyond their control. Just stop. Obviously, you can't stop in the middle of a thought (or can you?), so try to find a coda—some small observation or gesture—that will allow you to escape unnoticed.

ii) Starts and finishes are begun and ended unendingly. You might discover you've reached the ending in the second-to-last chapter and no longer need the last (William Shawn, long-time editor of *The New Yorker*, frequently removed the last paragraphs of stories). Or, you might complete a draft and still not find your first and last scenes until you've come some distance through the process of *rewriting*.

6. Rewriting — Again?

Hemingway's observation expresses the usual response a writer has to first drafts, the words lie bloated, lifeless on the page; they're the wrong words in the wrong order; and—wait a minute, they're not even your words. That's not your story; it's more like something written by a knucklehead, a dunce, a moron.

> "The first draft of anything is shit."
>
> —Ernest Hemingway

Film editor Ralph Rosenblum, in his movie memoir, *When the Shooting Stops...the Cutting Begins,* illustrates clearly the need to be ruthless during the editing process. In his case, it began with the movie's rough cut—usually one-third to one-half again longer than the finished version—lying on the screen like a beached whale. Mr. Rosenblum describes the movie-editing process as: removing scenes that don't move the story forward; hacking away at the ones remaining to sharpen their impact; then (if the filmmaker has money left) shooting additional scenes to fill in any narrative gaps.

> "The awful thing about the first sentence of any book is that as soon as you've written it you realize this piece of work is not going to be the great thing that you envisioned."
>
> — *Conversations with Tom Wolfe* [edited by Dorothy Scura]

The same principles apply to prose. Every writer has her or his own work method, although in that first draft, the compulsion to establish a narrative line—to know what the story is about—is all-consuming.

> "Omit needless words. Vigorous writing is concise. A sentence should contain no unnecessary words, a paragraph no unnecessary sentences… This requires not that the writer make all sentences short or avoid all detail and treat subjects only in outline, but that every word tell."
>
> —William Strunk, Jr. & E.B. White, *The Elements of Style*

A first draft rarely resembles the final one. Once completed, it will lie there, distended—a collection of pages (with impossibly diffuse words littering them) not resembling "that great thing you envisioned." That's when the removal of unnecessary words begins. As you cut and add, you'll see possible connections and shortcuts to tighten the narrative. Just remember, long manuscript = many cuts. Condense, condense, condense, until the story seems elliptical.

William Strunk's command—"Omit needless words"—is the essence of rewriting, and every word in your MS should drive the story forward. Rewriting always takes more time than that first draft, but, page-by-page, it is immensely satisfying for the writer to refine the work so that the prose whips the reader through the story.

> "I might write four lines or I might write twenty. I subtract and I add until I really hit something I want to do. You don't always whittle down, sometimes you whittle up."
>
> —Grace Paley

To do this, you need to be aware of your theme (which might have just become apparent), while streamlining the narrative and ensuring that the voice is consistent—what story are you trying to tell, and who is telling it (i.e. what voice)? Often those questions are answered as you rewrite.

Rough Draft	Revised Draft	Revised Draft with Dialogue
First Person, with clichés, little tension or conflict potential.	POV changed from First Person to Third Person Subjective.	Added specific, animate detail and dialogue.
It was a pleasant day with the birds singing and I felt as though my world were an oyster of my own picking. I felt lucky to be alive. It was my wedding day and by 2:00 that afternoon I would be married to Melissa, the most beautiful woman in the world. How could I have been so lucky as to meet such a beautiful woman? I smiled, remembering how we had met. I had been eating my lunch on a park bench and she had sat on the other end. She looked at me and was wondering, I guess, whom I might be but was more concerned with watching for her boyfriend. When he arrived, Rodrigo started shouting and she started crying. He called her nasty names and accused her of sleeping with his friend Alvaro whom she didn't know.	When she approached, he was eating his liverwurst on a bagel, as he did on the bench every day. The birds were singing. She had entered the park, glanced at him, and paced up and down the path before finally sitting on the far end of the bench. She was waiting for someone—a boyfriend? Why was she nervous? He had noted her short auburn hair which she kept hooking behind her ear. She hadn't even noted him. Eying the path, Robert wondered which man might be the lucky one. He had taken a bite of his sandwich when a black-haired 'dude' in a beige suit strode up, yelling at her. Robert heard the name Alvaro. She looked away, saying nothing. The 'dude' stopped. She said nothing. He told her he was disgusted with her and walked off. She sat quite	He was savouring the liverwurst and listening to birdsong as she entered the park. She glanced at him, paced up and down and finally perched on the far end of the bench, taking long meditative breaths. A black-haired 'dude' in a tight beige suit strode up and screamed at her, "You whore! When I find him, I'll eat his fucking balls." Robert almost choked on the bagel and, as he looked away, embarrassed, heard someone spit. "You disgust me," the 'dude' said, and left.

Robert glanced at the woman. Spittle ran down her cheek. She ignored him when he offered her his napkin, wiping her cheek with her sleeve. Awkwardly, he offered her half his liverwurst, but she didn't move, so he held out his grapes. She took one without thinking. |

Rough Draft	Revised Draft	Revised Draft with Dialogue
He told her he didn't want to ever see her again and walked off. When Melissa started crying, I didn't know what to do so I offered her half my lunch, which consisted of a bagel and cream cheese and some grapes which she declined, but it started a conversation about museums and I decided to not go back to work but to take her to one. We've now gone to a museum every day for the last two weeks, and I proposed to her in the Jansen Museum. She accepted and today is our wedding day. I'm really in love with her.	still. Robert waited quietly, then thought to offer her his napkin, until she looked at him, and he realized she wasn't crying. Then he offered her the rest of his bagel and liverwurst. She shook her head and he thought to hold out some grapes. She stared at him, and took one. She didn't move and he invited her to a museum. She accepted, and he did, not returning to work that day. Now, two weeks later, he was waiting happily on the same park bench, aware only at the last moment of the black-haired 'dude' striding up and smacking him across the face.	"There's a statue in the Jansen Museum," he said, abruptly, "of a woman whose child and husband were shot in war." He watched for her reaction. "What's remarkable is that her expression is defiant." She was watching him now, warily. "Would you like to see it?" he asked. After a moment, she nodded. That day, and every day for the next two weeks, he had watched her gaze intently at the statue. Now, on the park bench, waiting for her, Robert wondered if he still had his job, and what he might do for money. Only at the last moment was he aware of someone standing over him. "You suckhole," he heard just as a fist smashed into his face

Rewriting Considerations:

i) Keep detail to a minimum—any exposition must inform directly on the narrative or characters. Ask, "does the reader need this information now (i.e. if someone is dying, does it really matter what they're wearing?), and if so, how can it be woven into the narrative?"

> "When you catch an adjective, kill it. No, I don't mean utterly, but kill most of them—then the rest will be valuable. They weaken when they are close together. They give strength when they are wide apart."
> —Mark Twain

ii) Beware of extraneous details that take the reader out of the story. Run your sentences through a sieve. Trust the reader's imagination.

iii) Avoid the passive verb: e.g., change "He was terrified" to "He gaped at his trembling hands".

iv) Think always, "how does this scene contribute to the story?" Avoid forming attachments to scenes, images, dialogue, and memories that don't drive the narrative on. Each scene should contain enough incidents and specific, animate, character details to keep the story moving—if critical information is missing, other scenes will have to work harder to hold the reader's interest.

> "I rise at first light and I start by rereading and editing everything I have written to the point I left off. That way I go through a book I'm writing several hundred times. Most writers slough off the toughest but most important part of the trade—editing their stuff, honing it and honing it until it gets an edge like a bullfighter's killing sword."
> — Ernest Hemingway,
> *The Paris Review*

v) A reader can retain only so much and will lose interest if you describe everything. He or she wants to participate in creating the images, but excessive description smothers the imagination.

> "First drafts are for learning what your novel or story is about."
> —Bernard Malamud

vi)   The best metaphors sneak up on us. The fancy (hyper-extended) ones take the reader out of the story.

vii) Make your sentences lean and muscular so that the images you try to convey to the reader are sharp and vivid. Understand the intent and meaning of each word in your sentences and the order of the sentences in your paragraphs.

viii) Before rewriting it's helpful to remind yourself *of what to be continually aware.*

7. Of What to Be Continually Aware

Awareness changes daily. Any writer, living inside a mind full of shifting thoughts, plagued with doubt—though finding on rare occasions that life contains, as David Lynch once suggested, "little pears of euphoria"—must struggle each day to get to the nub of it. The following reminders might prove helpful:

1. *Subject* – Write about what interests you, no matter how outlandish. Don't be swayed by current literary trends. The Literati will offer suggestions as to what we *should* write; but the theme of your new project—the idea you might spend years working on—is what you feel *compelled* to write.

2. *Method* – Grab the reader by the throat, stoke the narrative incessantly with incident, preserve consistency of voice, and create character conflict, remembering to hide your theme beneath sparse dialogue and minimal, specific, animate character and setting detail.

3. *Narrative* – Look for incidents in character (and character in incidents) to hold the reader's attention, and for story-

"In any case, write what you know will always be excellent advice for those who ought not to write at all. Write what you think, what you imagine, what you suspect: that is the only way out of the dead end of the Serious Novel which so many ambitious people want to write and no one on earth—or even on campus—wants to read."

—Gore Vidal, "Thomas Love Peacock: The Novel of Ideas," *Essays: United States 1952-1992*

"When your Daemon is in charge, do not try to think consciously. Drift, wait and obey."

—Rudyard Kipling

lines to add to the narrative, weaving them in as unobtrusively as possible. Keep all narrative lines in motion to give the reader the sensation of travelling rapidly through a remote and fascinating, yet constantly changing, landscape.

4. *Less is More* – Don't be afraid of mystery. Not knowing keeps us reading, until eventually, making the connections, we experience that 'eureka' moment. The less we know, the more we want to find out. Any novelist who juggles character and incidents captivates the reader by raising questions (e.g. Why's he doing that? Why's she going there? etc.) and not answering them right away. From the first sentence on, tie the reader to your narrative with immediacy, action, a compelling voice, and by withholding unnecessary information. Offer just enough detail to keep the reader turning the page.

5. *Sex* – If you feel it necessary to include sex scenes in your work, ensure that they inform on either character or narrative (i.e. D.H. Lawrence). We've all seen sex—described by author Gore Vidal as "hydraulics"—graphically depicted in thousands of books, movies and TV shows, and it all looks the same. Sex has been commoditized. It plays to the lowest common denominator, and is used to attract the widest possible audience; there are no surprises left. Describing the sex act only becomes interesting when it moves the narrative forward or informs on the charac-

"She didn't obviously offer—what was it the fellow called it?—the promise of pneumatic bliss to the gentlemen with the sergeant-majors' horseshoe moustaches and gurglish voices!"

—Ford Maddox Ford, *Parade's End*

ters. Make the sex integral to the story, and present a fresh perspective, such as in *Sex for Fridge*, a short story by the Georgian author Zurab Lezhava (see *Recommended Short Prose*), a realistic and yet painfully funny depiction of the sex act.

> "Reality is not an inspiration for literature. At its best, literature is an inspiration for life."
> —Romain Gary

6. *Showing* – Show us, don't tell us. Telling me a character has a piercing headache isn't as compelling as showing that character writhing about, banging his or her head on the floor. Don't hesitate to put your characters into pain or danger. Peril compels us to read on. Showing generally allows us to believe what the author is saying. *Telling* me the man next door is strange doesn't impress me; *showing* him pissing on his neighbour's cat will.

> "Don't tell me the moon is shining. Show me the glint of light on the broken glass."
> — Anton Chekhov.

7. *Specific, animate detail (SAD)* – Start with an action, carefully adding detail, but ask, "does the exposition move the narrative forward?" If more detail is needed, and if it doesn't slow the narrative, salt it in as you go (showing us what the character is doing, wearing, eating, etc.) If there is an information gap, the reader's imagination will fill it in.

> "With sixty staring me in the face, I have developed inflammation of the sentence structure and a definite hardening of the paragraphs."
> —James Thurber

8. *Order of incident* – Among all the decisions a writer has to make (which scenes to show, which characters to include, etc.), the process by which you lead the reader into a scene can be critical.

What detail do you start with? Where do you want the character to end up in the scene, etc.?—i.e. if a baby is 'choking' *and* 'screaming' which do you put first? (Answer: 'screaming'—what a bystander would notice first).

9. *Quotation marks* – ("Always use quotation marks for dialogue," she commanded.) To indicate dialogue, some writers (e.g. James Joyce) have used dashes, and some nothing at all. Unfortunately, in millions of novels over the years, the reader has grown accustomed to dialogue in quotes (they are, after all, the characters' words being quoted). By avoiding them, the writer risks having the reader ask, "who's speaking?"

10. *Discouragement* – As you fumble through the first draft, incident by incident, it might seem as though nothing is happening. Keep in mind that the story *will* ramble until it's been rewritten many times. All narratives are assembled by the accumulation and elimination of incidents. Completing a draft, you'll see where the incidents and characters might converge and connect, glimpse how to add complexity to the characters, and tighten the structure. With any prose, but especially with a novel, it's useful to remember that any change in the narrative early on can lead to enormous repercussions for your characters later on.

> "I don't have a very clear idea of who the characters are until they start talking. Then I start to love them. By the time I finish the book, I love them so much that I want to stay with them. I don't want to leave them ever."
>
> —Joan Didion,
> *The Paris Review*

11. *Love your characters* – you can't spend hundreds of hours with your characters if you don't love them—after all, they are your creations. If you find yourself unable to love a

character, perhaps you've omitted a crucial detail. We're all vulnerable; we all have motives, experience pain and joy.

12. *Editing* – Cut, cut, cut. In early versions, we usually over-write. Cutting rejuvenates. Leave room for the reader's imagination. Cut with abandon (you can always put it back if you miss it). You'll know you're finished when there's nothing else to remove, and the narrative zips along.

> "In composing, as a general rule, run your pen through every other word you have written; you have no idea what vigor it will give to your style."
>
> —Sydney Smith

13. *Yakking* – Don't talk about your work *befo*re writing it (this is comparable to letting the steam out of a pressure cooker before the meat is cooked). And don't show your rough draft to anyone. If it is a *rough* draft, large chunks of what you hope to say will still be fermenting in your subconscious, and it's unlikely that whoever reads your MS will be able to visualize that great evocative work that you hope one day to complete. Some will

> "I just think it's bad to talk about one's present work, for it spoils something at the root of the creative act. It discharges the tension."
>
> —Norman Mailer

claim they'll be able to visualize your intent, but if at that moment *you* can't, how will *they*? If you join a writing workshop to discuss work *you've taken as far as you can*, it means that you have doubts, and are hoping for feedback from other writers. Some of the feedback will be of little use, but, in revisiting your work through the eyes of others, you might make new discoveries.

14. *DL* – When confronted with Dead Language look for a new expression, or turn an old one around. The Irish

"Whatever has been well said by anyone is mine."

—Seneca

writer Sean O'Faolain once wrote a short story in which the character's eyes "helicoptered around the room," a phrase precisely describing the character's mindset at that moment.

15. *Listening* – Listen intently to the conversations around you. You will be buried in heaps of dead language but you might also catch original turns of phrase.

16. *In other words* – We all forget words. Buy a Roget's. The use of a thesaurus is indispensable to anyone wanting to have the exact word at hand in order to formulate clear, forceful, and succinct prose.

17. *Get it down* – When you attempt your first draft, don't concern yourself with dead language (plenty will have crept into your sentences); all you're trying to accomplish is to lay out a narrative for your potentially compelling story. Once you have a draft, no matter how it wanders, you'll be able to glimpse a narrative line much more clearly. Then, in the rewriting, remove the dead words.

"Once you've got some words looking back at you, you can take two or three—throw them away and look for others."

—Bernard Malamud

18. *Rules* – Consider learning a few before you break them.

8. Rules – Must We Obey?

Most writers create their own rules, some quite idiosyncratic; most intersecting. George Orwell's six rules for writing are often paraphrased and recommended by others.

Rules by Elmore Leonard and Kurt Vonnegut also have useful guidelines to offer, and OUR list of rules, derived mostly from experience and reading, contains many similarities. In most cases, Orwell, Leonard, or Vonnegut have expressed the rule more succinctly; and in some cases we don't necessarily agree (e.g. Elmore's No. 3).

Here's what guides us:

> "There are three rules for writing a novel. Unfortunately, no one knows what they are."
>
> —Somerset Maugham, *Maybe You Should Write a Book*, Ralph Daigh.

GEORGE ORWELL's Six Rules for Writing		
	1.	Never use a metaphor, simile or other figure of speech which you are used to seeing in print.
	2.	Never use a long word where a short one will do.
	3.	If it is possible to cut out a word, always cut it out.
	4.	Never use the passive where you can use the active.
	5.	Never use a foreign phrase, a scientific word or a jargon word if you can think of an everyday English equivalent.
	6.	Break any of these rules sooner than say anything outright barbarous.
ELMORE LEONARD's Ten Rules of Writing	1.	Never open a book with weather.
	2.	Avoid prologues.
	3.	Never use a verb other than "said" to carry dialogue.
	4.	Never use an adverb to modify the verb "said".
	5.	Keep your exclamation points under control.

ELMORE LEONARD's Ten Rules of Writing (suite)	6. Never use the words "suddenly" or "all hell broke loose." 7. Use regional dialect, patois, sparingly. 8. Avoid detailed descriptions of characters. 9. Don't go into great detail describing places and things. 10. Try to leave out the part that readers tend to skip; and, if it sounds like writing, rewrite it.
KURT VONNEGUT'S 'Creative Writing 101'	1. Use the time of a total stranger in such a way that he or she will not feel the time was wasted. 2. Give the reader at least one character he or she can root for. 3. Every character should want something, even if it is only a glass of water. 4. Every sentence must do one of two things—reveal character or advance the action. 5. Start as close to the end as possible. 6. Be a sadist. No matter how sweet and innocent your leading characters, make awful things happen to them—in order that the reader may see what they are made of. 7. Write to please just one person. If you open a window and make love to the world, so to speak, your story will get pneumonia. 8. Give your readers as much information as possible as soon as possible. To hell with suspense. Readers should have such complete understanding of what is going on, where and why, that they could finish the story themselves, should cockroaches eat the last few pages.
OUR Rules for Writing	a. Avoid clichés. Familiarity breeds contempt. Any cliché will place your prose among the commonplace. b. "Omit unnecessary words." (Strunk) c. Never use a hyper-extended metaphor or simile. d. Never use the passive verb when you can use the active. e. Never open a book with description—weather, scenery, wardrobe or otherwise (unless you're Charles Dickens). f. Use exclamation points and question marks sparingly?! g. Don't plug dialogue with exposition. h. Avoid beginning with: prologues, forewords, introductions, etc. Get right to your narrative, and your protagonist's emotional reality. Any necessary info can be salted in as you go. i. More guts on the page. j. Rewrite your prose until it's as smooth as a ~~baby's bottom~~ giraffe's bum.

a.   **Avoid clichés** – in his book *On Cliches*, Dutch sociologist Anton C. Zijderveld, suggests that all clichés are forms of human expression (written, oral, etc.) which, because of repetition, have lost their "heuristic" ability—their power to represent.

> "Do not pay any attention to the rules other people make... they make them for their own protection, and to hell with them."
>
> —William Saroyan

Clichés are largely common in pop culture (i.e. how did the word 'cool'—slang used by the relatively small number of jazz musicians in the 40s and 50s—become ubiquitous and senseless in our present-day, industrial society?).

Clichés usually indicate that the writer has a limited vocabulary, a tired imagination, or is unable to describe complex emotions and transitions. The use of clichés inhibits the creation of strong prose (see Dead Language), their dull familiarity sending the reader to sleep. When consciously confronted by a cliché you've just written, try experimenting with a word or expression never used before in that context (e.g. "heart pounding" could become "heart drumming" or "heart clacking like a freight train" or "heart reporting," "heart stomping"). To illustrate what's possible, here are two examples of original turns of phrase by Evelyn Waugh, who, in a journalism piece early in his career, found a vivid and original way to describe the arrival of autumn: "...there are brown leaves in the squares and the smell of bonfires and, on our way to dinner, an unsuspected draughtiness about the windows of the motor car."

> "Blot out, correct, insert, refine,
> Enlarge, diminish, interline;
> Be mindful, when invention fails,
> To scratch your head, and bite your nails."
>
> —Jonathan Swift

And, in *Brideshead Revisited*, to illustrate the protagonist's sexual attraction to another character: "...as I took the cigarette from my lips and put it in hers, I caught a thin bat's squeak of sexuality, inaudible to any but me."

b. **Omit needless words** – This mantra ~~directive by William Strunk Jr. is~~ to be strictly obeyed. ~~You will always over-write in~~ ~~The first draft is always overwritten because~~ You're still ~~working out what you're trying to say~~ creating in that first draft, using many more words than are necessary to express your idea. Re-writing ~~then becomes a an intriguing~~ challenges you to rake ~~ing through the work to clean~~ away the deadwood ~~useless words~~.

c. **Never use a hyper-extended metaphor or simile** – it's baffling whenever a complicated metaphor or simile is held as high as King Kong on the Empire State Building to signify literary achievement when these ten-tonne trucks loaded down with overly-wrought figures of speech slam into the wall of comprehension, forcing the reader to decipher their meaning.

> "All metaphor breaks down somewhere. That is the beauty of it. It is touch and go with the metaphor, and until you have lived with it long enough you don't know when it is going. You don't know how much you can get out of it and when it will cease to yield. It is a very living thing. It is as life itself."
>
> —Robert Frost, "Education by Poetry," *The Selected Prose of Robert Frost*

d. **Use the active verb** – "I was angry with her at that moment" is not as active as "I hated her then." Omit the passive verb and you tighten the writing a notch. Don't tell us—"I was depressed"—show the character moaning with despair.

e. **Never start a story with description**—weather, scenery, wardrobe, or otherwise – on page one, the reader isn't interested in the green-shaded stream which meandered through the Town of—, past the Fire Station (its red walls signifying danger), past the park where children ran playing among the maple trees and lingered at the fountain; or the russet leaves of autumn lying like dead soldiers on the grass in the city park; or the sullen, grey sky blanketing the sea's horizon, the clouds crossing the heavens like ships on the strait; or the drab, dark, red brick streets of the factory town; or the patterns of soft rain-drizzle bouncing on the tarmac. The reader wants to know who and what. Who is the story about; and what is going to happen to her or him—what obstacles face the protagonist; and what is he or she going to do about it? Once you've hooked the reader, you can seed in the specific, animate detail. (Keep those bookstore browsers in mind, stalking the shelves for a story that will capture them immediately.)

> "Whatever you can do or dream you can, begin it;
> Boldness has genius, power and magic in it."
> — Johann Wolfgang von Goethe

f. **Avoid exclamation points!! And question marks??** – Any overuse of a literary symbol is annoying—these in particular! Aren't they irritating when used frequently?! Yes! Most definitely! Almost always!!!

> "An exclamation point is like laughing at your own joke."
> —F. Scott Fitzgerald

g. **Don't plug dialogue with exposition** – Using dialogue to convey summary exposition (back-story) creates:

  i. false-sounding dialogue which prevents the characters from coming alive in the reader's imagination;

  ii. scenes with little or no action, which stall the narrative;

    iii. too many answers—too much information. The reader reads on only out of curiosity to find out "why are they doing that?" or, "why is she behaving strangely?"

h.   **Avoid prologues** – Any writing placed before the actual beginning of a narrative seems, to us, pointless, redundant, or self-conscious—a flood of expository text through which the reader needs to wade to reach the narrative. A prologue (introduction, foreword, etc.) blocks the reader from entering the story right away, raising distracting questions: Is this the real story? Why does the writer feel they need to prep the story for me with a prologue? *And why is it in italics?* At the beginning, your reader is struggling to suspend disbelief. Begin the *real* story immediately. Any incidents, details, or characters in your prologue or foreword—if they're essential—can be woven into the main narrative.

> "Context is all. And a relatively pure heart. Relatively pure—for if you had a pure heart you wouldn't be in the book-writing business in the first place."
> —Robert Penn Warren

i.   **More guts on the page** – to hold the reader's attention, keep the emotions of your characters raw and exposed. Compelling fiction is tightly connected to what's hidden just beneath the surface.

j.   **If it sounds like writing, rewrite it** – this is Elmore Leonard's final recommendation and is reinforced by these quotes by Orwell: "And yet it is also true that one can write nothing readable unless one constantly struggles to efface one's personality. Good prose is like a window pane." And Johnson: "Read over your compositions, and wherever you meet with a passage which you think is particularly fine, strike it out."

The exception proves the rule. Dickens' opening to *Bleak House*—an endless description of English fog (page 103)—violates rule 'e', but is so pervasive and captivating that he pulls it off.

> "Any fool can make a rule and every fool will mind it."
> —Henry David Thoreau

"It is a fact that few novelists enjoy the creative labour, though most enjoy thinking about the creative labour."—Arnold Bennett

9. The Creative Process – What Is It?

Good question.

Neurological science has only partial theories to suggest where our intuitive processes originate. According to biologist E.O. Wilson "The human brain is the most complex system, either organic or inorganic, known in the universe." It defies understanding, and science has not, as yet, penetrated its great mystery.

What we do know is that our imaginations are infinite, so why would anyone set out to write with limited aspirations? As Stephen King suggests: "People who decide to make a fortune writing like John Grisham or Tom Clancy produce nothing but pale imitations, by and large, because vocabulary is not the same thing as feeling and plot is light-years from the truth as it is understood by *the mind and the heart.*" [italics ours]

Life has no plot (although death is a 'killer' ending), yet an original narrative with the slightest miscellany of character and incidents can present us with an entirely fresh and bracing view of existence. Many of the great novels (e.g.

"The story, the plot of a novel is of no interest to me. When I write a novel I aim at rendering a colour, a shade. For instance, in my Carthaginian novel, I want to do something purple. The rest, the characters and the plot is a mere detail. In Madame Bovary, all I wanted to do was to render a grey colour, the mouldy colour of a wood-louse's existence. The story of the novel mattered so little to me that a few day's before starting on it I still had in mind a very different Madame Bovary from the one I created: the setting and the overall tone were the same, but she was to have been a chaste and devout old maid. And then I realized that she would have been an impossible character."

—Gustave Flaubert as quoted in *The Brothers Goncourt Diaries*

Ulysses, The Idiot, Moby Dick) are plot-less, the reader drawn through those works by narrative comprised of fragments of vaguely-related events, which seem to arrive from the unconscious mind.

"Einstein suggested that the creative scientists are the ones with access to their dreams... As Freud realized, in establishing his distinction between primary and secondary process thought, the mind is capable of functioning both intuitively and according to the dictates of common sense. The implication of Einstein's remark is that, in order to innovate, the scientist, like anyone else, must break the grip on his imagination that our powers of logical-seeming storytelling impose."
—*The Oxford Companion to the Mind*

'Thinking' appears to occur in the brain's two cerebral halves—the Right and Left hemispheres—which, along with the lobes (the Occipital, the Parietal, the Temporal, and the Frontal), the cerebellum and all other parts of the nervous system, control all functions of the body. These two hemispheres are considered the source of some or all of our 'creative' thoughts.

It is assumed that the Left controls rational, logical, and analytical thought, leading to problem-solving (e.g. mathematics), story-telling, and a talent for detail; while the Right is responsible for creative, spatial, intuitive thought (e.g. painting), talented at free association, and possibly has something to do with dream-work.

All the information received by the mind is stored in neurons—some ten billion or so—in both hemispheres and the lobes. Exactly how we access the thoughts in our neurons is not yet clear. Diane Ackerman, in her book *An Alchemy of Mind*, reminds us that Proust believed that our memories resided inside objects, and were only released to us by direct and unexpected contact, so that the scent of a pine forest or the taste of a coconut macaroon or the sudden shifting light in a grey sky could connect us instantly to memories stored in those neurons.

The Right and Left hemispheres communicate with each other through a cranial cable, a thick network of fibres (of up to eight hundred million) called the corpus callosum. Yet, how exactly the two brains converse is uncertain.

> "Writing is no trouble: you just jot down ideas as they occur to you. The jotting is simplicity itself—it's the occurring which is difficult."
> —Stephen Leacock

We do know that those who practice Zen Buddhism set out to achieve a balance of activity between both hemispheres, which the Buddhists see as strong mental health or 'satori' (enlightenment). Would this 'balance' serve the writer, given that the most affecting writing is thought to come from our neuroses?

Many books on writing instruct the reader on how to invent plot, setting and characters. This methodology—in *consciously* presupposing what the story will be—uses the Left Brain predominantly to create the story *before the writer even begins writing it.*

Unfortunately, the left brain seems able only to offer up logical, received ideas (i.e. boy meets girl, man fights for justice, revenge, etc.), tending to ignore the turbulent possibilities that hover on the edge of the writer's imagination—those serendipitous scraps retained (or generated) by the right brain. The Left Brain gives us plot *without free association*; consequently, the writing, using familiar situations and resolutions, can resemble a 'paint-by-numbers' approach. There are few surprises. Much genre writing—romance, western, fan-

> "Keep your bones in good motion, kid, and quietly consume and digest what is necessary. I think it is not so much important to build a literary thing as it is not to hurt things. I think it is important to be quiet and in love with park benches; solve whole areas of pain by walking across a rug."
> —Charles Bukowski

tasy, thriller, etc.—would appear to be Left Brain-oriented. This is not to say that genre can't transcend the analytical power of the Left Brain—it can, but it does require access to the free associations of the Right Brain. Imaginative prose requires logic, but, more importantly, it must have dream-time to allow the unfettered flow of original memory fragments to surface.

Science still is uncertain as to where these 'fragments' are stored. The temporal lobe? The unconscious mind? What exactly is the unconscious mind, and where does it reside in the brain? And what role does it play in the creative process?

"Follow the accident, fear the fixed plan—that is the rule."
—John Fowles

What we've imagined is that creative thought arrives from a kind of industrial complex, consisting of a factory (Left Brain) and a warehouse (Right Brain). In the warehouse, a guy named Bob supervises storage of all the raw material—the cognitive flotsam and jetsam of your inner life. Bob, fortunately, is lackadaisical, and not concerned with organizing the stored images and sounds, which are continually pouring in from all senses. He spends his day (while listening to Mahler on his I-pod and reading Elmore Leonard novels) bulldozing the piles of memory fragments into the back corners of the warehouse to make room for all the new cognitive sludge pouring in. Then, whenever the sheer volume of mental refuse defeats him, Bob simply shoves it down the corpus callosum to the factory.

In the factory, Betty, the supervisor at the tunnel's other end, is constantly unsettled by Bob's lack of fastidiousness, and overwhelmed by the sheer amount of mind-detritus he sends to her. She keeps trying to arrange a meeting with Bob with the hope of scheduling a methodology, but Bob, preoccupied with his reading and music, ignores her.

When the writer's creative 'juices' are flowing, Bob and Betty are both hard at work; Bob shoving the overflow of thought-rubbish down the chute to the factory where Betty struggles to create order. Your night and day dreams are likely a result of Betty not being able to cope with all the fragments coming down the chute from Bob.

Betty was perfectly happy creating your novel on her own, working with what she had stored in the factory. Yet because of Bob's lackadaisical approach, she's forced to construe a narrative from all the cognitive refuse flooding in. Could your seemingly nonsensical 'dreams' (e.g. being arrested for punching out a politician resembling your father; sleeping with your finger in your ear to prevent your wife from cleaning your ear drum; being kicked in the shin by your ex-employer for refusing to give *her* a reference; touring Ireland with a lover you dumped who's now dumping *you*; being attacked in the bath by mangy dogs belonging to your ex-wife or husband; having Oprah interrogate you about your voluminous paranormal sex novel; or being pursued by Bill Gates through a warehouse, stacked high with old PCs) be the creative process in full throttle?

> "There is hardly any distinction between a writer and a journalist—indeed, most writers *are* journalists. Nothing wrong with journalism any more than with dentistry, but they are worlds apart! Whenever I read the English Sunday papers I notice that the standard of literacy is high—all very clever and hollow—but no dues to literature. They care about their own egos. They synopsize the book, tell the plot. Well, fuck the plot! That is for precocious schoolboys. What matters is the imaginative *truth*, and the perfection and care with which it has been rendered."
> —Edna O'Brien, *The Paris Review*

> "It's nervous work. The state you need to write in is the state that others are paying huge sums to get rid of."
> —Shirley Hazzard

It also works in reverse. Sometimes Bob, irked by Betty's efficiency, decides that he will write the novel himself, bulldozing hundreds of memory fragments into a pile. Intriguing, odd, inexplicable, quirky, disparate incidents emerge, but no narrative. Eventually Bob gives up and sends it all down the tunnel to where Betty struggles to sort the psychic sludge into theme, narrative, voice, setting, characters, dialogue and syntax.

"If life be delayed till interest and envy are at an end, we may hope for impartiality, but must expect little intelligence; for the incidents which give excellence to biography are of a volatile and evanescent kind, such as soon escape the memory."

—Samuel Johnson

In the factory, ultimately, Betty tells the characters what the story is; when Bob and his warehouse are actively involved, the characters tell Betty. In other words, *plot* is imposed on the characters, *narrative* is what actually happens to them, and is more persuasive to the reader because *it resembles real life.*

Questions abound. What is memory? What is the subconscious? And where do they live, in the Right or Left Brain, or in the corpus callosum, or somewhere as yet undetected? And where exactly does the imagination reside?

It seems essential that the mind be allowed to play. Both hemispheres are needed to write 'creatively'; but the process seems to begin in the Right Brain. The odd bits of detritus of your life— those memory fragments—accessed through the Right Brain, are what gives your writing the sense of being rooted in reality.

"One must avoid ambition in order to write. Otherwise something else is the goal: some kind of power beyond the power of language. And the power of language, is seems to me, is the only kind of power a writer is entitled to."

—Cynthia Ozick

This reliance on the Right Brain means that you will not consciously know, to begin with, what you're writing about or how it will end, which—we think—is how fiction works best and is borne out by the following writers:

E.L. Doctorow

"...nevertheless I say that no matter what your plan or inspiration, or trembling recognition for an idea that you know belongs to you, the strange endowment you set loose by the act of writing is never entirely under your control. It cannot be a matter solely of willed expression. Somewhere from the depths of your being you find a voice: it is the first and most mysterious moment of the creative act. There is no book without it. If it takes off, it appears to you self-governed. To some degree you will write to find out what you are writing. And you feel no sense of possession for what comes onto the pages—what you experience is a sense of discovery." —*Creationists*

Isaac Asimov

"In the old days, when I was writing a great deal of fiction, there would come, once in a while, moments when I was stymied. Suddenly, I would find I had written myself into a hole and could see no way out. To take care of that, I developed a technique which invariably worked. It was simply this—I went to the movies. Not just any movie. I had to pick a movie which was loaded with action but which made no demands on the intellect. As I watched, I did my best to avoid any conscious thinking concerning my problem, and when I came out of the movie I knew exactly what I would have to do to put the story back on track. It never failed... It is my belief, you see, that thinking is a double phenomenon like breathing." [*The Eureka Phenomenon*].

"I've always figured the only way I could finish a book and get a plot was just to keep making it longer and longer until something happens— you know, until it finds its own plot—because you can't outline and then fit the thing into it. I suppose it's a slow way of working."

—Nelson Algren, *The Paris Review*

Ray Bradbury

Ray Bradbury described his writing technique as lying in bed awake early in the morning, hearing voices in his head, then jumping up and running to his desk to get them down before they faded.

Robert Frost

"Every time a poem is written, every time a short story is written, it is written not by cunning, but by belief. The beauty, the something, the little charm of the thing to be, is more felt than known. There is a common jest, one that always annoys me, on the writers, that they write the last end first, and then work up to it; that they lay a train toward one sentence that they think is pretty nice and have all fixed up to set a trap to close with. No, it should not be that way at all. No one who has ever come close to the arts has failed to see the difference between the thing written that way, with cunning and device, and the kind that are believed into existence, that begin in something more felt than known." — Robert Frost, *Education by Poetry*

> "Health is the ability to stand in the spaces between realities without losing any of them. This is what I believe self-acceptance means and what creativity is really all about— the capacity to feel like one self while being many."
> —Philip M. Bromberg, *Standing in the Spaces: Essays in Clinical Process, Trauma, and Dissociation*

Anthony Burgess

"No novelist who has created a credible personage can ever be quite sure what that personage will do. Create your characters, give them a time and place to exist in, and leave the plot to them; the imposing of action on them is very difficult, since action must spring out of the temperament with which you have endowed them. At best there will be a compromise between the narrative line you have dreamed up and the course of action preferred by the characters. Finally, though, it will seem that action is there to illustrate character; it is character that counts." — *Ninety-Nine Novels: The Best in English since 1939* — *A Personal Choice*, Anthony Burgess

Joan Didion

On her novel, *The Book of Common Prayer.*

'I knew why Charlotte went to the airport even if Victor did not. I knew about airports.'

"This 'I' was the voice of no author in my house. This 'I' was someone who not only knew why Charlotte went to the airport but also knew someone called 'Victor.' Who was Victor? Who was this narrator? Why was this narrator telling me this story? Let me tell you one thing about why writers write: had I known the answer to any of these questions I would never have needed to write a novel."

And...

"Poets do not go mad; but chess players do. Mathematicians go mad, and cashiers; but creative artists very seldom. I am not, as will be seen, in any sense attacking logic: I only say that this danger does lie in logic, not in imagination."

—G.K. Chesterton

"I began *Play It as It Lays* just as I have begun each of my novels, with no notion of "character" or "plot" or even "incident." I had only two pictures in my mind... and a technical intention, which was to write a novel so elliptical and fast that it would be over before you noticed it, a novel so fast that it would scarcely exist on the page at all." —Joan Didion, *Why I Write*

Graham Greene

"In the far longer work of the novel there were periods of great weariness, but at any moment the unexpected might happen—a minor character would suddenly take control and dictate his words and actions. Somewhere near the beginning, for no reason I knew, I would insert an incident which seemed entirely irrelevant, and sixty thousand words later, with a sense of excitement, I would realize why it was there—the narrative had been working all that time outside my conscious control." — *Ways of Escape*

"For Christ sake write and don't worry what the boys will say nor whether it will be a masterpiece nor what. I write one page of masterpiece to ninety-one pages of shit. I try to put the shit in the wastebasket... forget your personal tragedy. We are all bitched from the start and you especially have to be hurt like hell before you can write seriously."
—Ernest Hemingway

Stephen King

"I distrust plot for two reasons: first, because our *lives* are largely plotless, even when you add in all our reasonable precautions and careful planning; and second, because I believe plotting and the spontaneity of real creation aren't compatible. It's best that I be as clear about this as I can—I want you to understand that my basic belief about the making of stories is that they pretty much make themselves. The job of the writer is to give them a place to grow... Plot is, I think, the good writer's last resort, and the dullard's first choice. The story which results from it is apt to feel artificial and laboured... Story is honourable and trustworthy; plot is shifty, and best kept under house arrest." — *On Writing*

John Cheever

"I don't work with plots. I work with intuition, apprehension, dreams, concepts. Characters and events come simultaneously to me. Plot implies narrative and a lot of crap. It's a calculated attempt to hold the reader's interest at the sacrifice of moral conviction. Of course, one doesn't want to be boring... one needs an element of suspense. But a good narrative is a rudimentary structure, rather like a kidney." —*The Paris Review*

William Kennedy

"Who cares about the plot? Who? Forster in *The Art of the Novel* dismissed it as a faintly contemptible thing you have to have, somehow, but that's really not where the story exists. The character does something which is new, and then the story begins to percolate. If I knew at the beginning how the book was going to end, I would probably never finish. I knew that Legs Diamond was going to die at the end of the book [*Legs*], so I killed him on page one." —*The Paris Review*

> "I write the big scenes first, that is, the scenes that carry the meaning of the book, the emotional experience."
>
> —Joyce Cary, *The Paris Review*

And from two writers prominent during the golden age of British television drama (1960s – 1980s):

Dennis Potter

"I never have a plot. I don't have a schema... I either have one image, or I may have a sense of where the image has got to be, and then find that it hasn't got to be there at all, which is always the best feeling. Then I write—and I write extremely intensely, hour upon hour until I'm exhausted, because I'm frightened of losing it when I'm doing it. I hate starting it, too. I hate the process...

"There are writers... I presume, who work out everything before they sit down to put the words in order. For me... writing... is more like pulling and pulling and pulling on a string that already has its weights attached, or dipping a thimble again and again into a pool that was already there.

"The effort, the curiosity, the surprise or the anxiety are each strong enough so to fill the mind there is no room for 'thought'..." —*Dennis Potter: A Biography*, Humphrey Carpenter

"To develope [sic] at all as a writer I have to develope [sic] in my own way. The 108 pages are very angular and awkward but a great deal of that can be corrected when I have finished the rest of it—and only then. I will not be hurried or directed by Rinehart. I think they are interested in the conventional and I have had no indication that they are very bright."

—Flannery O'Connor, *The Habit of Being, the Letters of Flannery O'Connor* [Ed. Sally Fitzgerald]

(Letter to Paul Engle, a former teacher, in regard to *Wise Blood*. Rinehart was the first publisher to express interest in the material).

David Mercer

"I don't know what my next play will be like, or about, and shan't know until I am at least halfway through it. The first impulse springs from an accumulation of images, tensions, fragments. The only rational problem is to find that cohering thread which will lead to an overall statement." —*Dennis Potter: A Biography*, Humphrey Carpenter

So how does the novice writer begin a work of prose? Oddly enough, the secret to exploring the depths of your imagination is to be found in one of the earliest (1823) of the How to Write books, *The Art of Becoming an Original Writer in Three Days*, by Ludwig Börne.

Börne's suggestion is simplicity itself. "Take several sheets of paper and for three days in succession, without any pretence or hypocrisy, write down everything that comes to your mind. Write what you think about yourself, about women, about the Turkish War, about Goethe… about the Last Judgment, about your boss—and after three days you will be beside yourself with surprise at all the new, unheard-of-ideas you had. That's the art of becoming an original writer in three days!"

Try not to force logical thoughts upon your narrative and your characters. Let Bob in his own shambling way start the process, bulldozing those thought-scraps down the chute to Betty, who even now is striving to create order.

10. The Writer's Mission

As writer, you are sovereign. No one can (or should) tell you what to write. You live in the free society of your own mind—all that goopy, psychic sludge is yours—and if you've spent days, weeks, months, possibly years, pulling stories from it, it is comprised of your sweat, tears and innermost thoughts.

"I write in order to achieve that feeling of tension relieved and function achieved which a cow enjoys on giving milk."
—H.L. Mencken

In the publishing trade, you might encounter certain "in the know" types who will readily offer up input on the form your next work should take (i.e. a multi-generational, ethnic family drama; or, the historical saga of an Asian immigrant who, working hard to succeed against impossible odds and opposition, opens a successful restaurant / laundry / IT consultancy; or, the story of a woman who overcomes abortion, heart disease, breast cancer, and a sex change operation to become Leader of the Liberal Party).

"When you meet a master swordsman, show him your sword.
When you meet a man who is not a poet, do not show him your poem."
—Zen Koan

Ignore current trends. Listen instead to that insistent voice inside your skull—Bob sending memory scraps through the corpus callosum to Betty, inadvertently providing the raw material for what you feel compelled to write next.

"I occasionally have an anti-Roth reader in mind. I think, 'how he is going to hate this.' That can be just the encouragement I need."

—Philip Roth,
The Paris Review

Be aware that if you are writing instinctively, and offering up unpopular criticisms, you will take flak for it, or be ignored. Both conditions are unsettling until you realize that acceptance by the mob is not necessarily a favoured state of being—such a condition might mean that your work is mediocre. As a writing student once observed, "is anything popular ever interesting?" Innovations by those who push the envelope are never greeted with alacrity by the mob until someone says, "This is genius!"

As John Steinbeck once instructed a young writer:

"You have to assume that the act of writing is the most important of all. If you start worrying about people's feelings, then you get nowhere..."

—Norman Mailer,
The Paris Review

"I'm sorry you had an argument with your father. But from where I sit, and I sit a little bit along the road you are travelling, you have only one thing in the world to do. You must finish this book and then you must finish another. If anything at all—saving your own death—stops you, except momentarily, then you are not a writer anyway and there is nothing to discuss. I do not mean that you should not bitch and complain and fight and scrabble but the one important thing for you is to get your work done. If anyone gets hurt in the process, you cannot be blamed.

"The fact that many people should be shocked by what he writes practically imposes it as a duty upon the writer to go on shocking them."

—Aldous Huxley

"But don't think for a moment that you will ever be forgiven for being what they call 'different.' You won't! I still have not been forgiven. Only when I am delivered in a pine box will I be considered 'safe.' After I had written *The Grapes of Wrath* and it had been to a large extent read and sometimes burned, the librarians at Salinas Public Library, who had known my folks, remarked that it was lucky my parents were dead so that they did not have to suffer this shame. I tell you this so you may know what to expect. Now get to work." —(*Steinbeck, A Life in Letters*)

There should be no one between you and the paper. It's your story and you decide what goes into it. You might want input, you might not; it's your decision. *You* live with the work. While others go for lunch, you're sweating over the blank page.

You're the writer.

> "There is no doubt about it, in the Twentieth century
> if you are to come to be writing really writing
> you cannot make a living at it no not by writing."
> —Gertrude Stein

"My father said I was the ugliest child he had ever seen. He told me that all his life and I believed him. And I'd accepted that nobody would ever love me. But do you know, nobody cares what a writer looks like. I could write to be eighty and be grotesque... and that wouldn't matter. For me, writing was an act of love. It was an attempt not to get the world's attention, it was an attempt to be loved."

—James Baldwin

11. Glossary

a. *Arc* – the line of the narrative, the word 'arc' suggesting a dramatic curve or trajectory, as opposed to a dull, flat line.

b. *Canlit* – a school of rural and historical writing from English Canada, having to do with Canadians overcoming and embracing snow, ice, forests, oceans, mountains, prairies, and other animals; a genre now examing our multicultural, multisexual mosaic.

c. *Character* – a collection of intriguing physical, mental, social (or sociopathic) human traits.

d. *Compelled ones* – writers self-coerced, perpetually scribbling.

e. *Dead language* – words and phrases mis- and overused to the degree that they no longer contain sense or meaning.

f. *Editor* – can be helpful (often inadvertently), but occasionally fails to bridle the writer's genius.

g. *Erotica* – endless wordy descriptions of human hydraulics.

"Mostly, we authors must repeat ourselves—that's the truth. We have two or three great moving experiences in our lives—experiences so great and moving that it doesn't seem at the time that anyone else has been caught up and pounded and dazzled and astonished and beaten and broken and rescued and illuminated and rewarded and humbled in just that way ever before."

—F. Scott Fitzgerald

"Editors know best what they want when they open up a manuscript and find it right there in front of them."

—Stanley Ellin

h.   *Hyper-extended metaphor or simile* – a metaphor or simile taken beyond its breaking point by an image so bizarre, striking, and confusing (e.g. "Susan sank into the sofa, its springs thrusting out like the ribs of a hungry wolf") that the image smothers the original thought.

i.   *Literary Agent* – The occasional sales of a book to foreign territories by these canny folk fills the writer with expectation, until the agent offers a critical market analysis of the author's current MS.

j.   *Literary Awards* – Glittering events at which writers, fêted with free meat and drink, given media attention, statues and money, begin to wonder, "is this me?"

k.   *Literati* – the cognoscenti of the book world.

l.   *Marketing* – a department in a publishing concern run by enthusiastic young people with degrees in Business, Communication or Marketing, who spend their days speculating what the next 'breakout' book will be.

> "Most writers are not quick-witted when they talk. Novelists, in particular, drag themselves around in society like gut-shot bears."
>
> —Kurt Vonnegut,
> *The Paris Review*

m.   *Memoir* – a work of 'true' prose by someone describing their time on Planet Earth—a shout of "I was there."

n.   *Metaphor* – if being considered, should be used sparingly and slightly so as not to stun the reader (see excerpt from Gabriella Goliger's short story *Maedele*, (page 33).

o.   *Narrative* – incidents and character; character and incidence.

p.   *Novel* – comes from the Italian *novella* 'tale, piece of news' from the Latin *novus*, new.

q. *Novice* – an author who seeks applause for his or her prose but not at the cost of working to improve it.

r. *Poetry* – from the Greek poētēs, meaning doer or creator.

> "I can't understand these chaps who go around American Universities explaining how they write poems: it's like going round explaining how you sleep with your wife."
>
> —Philip Larkin, *The Paris Review*

s. *POV (Point of View)* – the voice of the storyteller. Sometimes confused with Multiple POV Disorder, a contagious but not incurable affliction that renders authors unable to sustain a narrative line from a single point of view.

t. *Producer* – A non-writer who knows how to get movies made and who therefore assumes (erroneously) that he knows how to make them.

u. *Prologue* – a baffling chunk of prose— *often in italics*—placed at the beginning of a work, seemingly unrelated to the main plot, and intended to signify complexity, meaning, and profundity.

> "No author is a man of genius to his publisher."
>
> —Heinrich Heine

v. *Publisher* – Always keen and helpful, able to point out severe problems in the writer's manuscript (wrong protagonist, characters, or events), but most encouraging while waiting for the writer to offer free revisions.

w. *Right of First Refusal* – a contractual clause in a contract, allowing a publisher or movie producer the opportunity to evaluate your work before you offer it to someone who might actually buy it.

x. *Screenplay* – a plaything for producers and other non-writers—solitary confinement and masochism for writers.

> "One must have a heart of stone to read the death of Little Nell by Dickens without laughing."
>
> —Oscar Wilde

y.   *Setting* – the physical, political, emotional, or ethereal atmosphere in which a story can occur (see *The Third Policeman*).

z.   *Simile* – a metaphor using 'as' or 'like' to introduce it. Not to be confused with Valley Girl-Speak.

aa.   *Slush Pile* – an age-old device for finding new work, made redundant by publishers' accounting departments. Although some successful novelists and books (e.g. Philip Roth, *Diary of Anne Frank, Ordinary People*) were saved from the slush pile, many publishers no longer accept unsolicited manuscripts. They might consider reinstating this useful practice. By employing two or three college students—those majoring in history or philosophy (not English)—to vet unsolicited submissions during the summer vacation, it would take only one slush-pile best-seller to make the exercise viable.

> "In anything fit to be called by the name of reading, the process itself should be absorbing and voluptuous; we should gloat over a book, be rapt clean out of ourselves."
>
> —Robert Louis Stevenson

bb.   *Story* – the narrative line running through the tale that places the reader inside the protagonist's emotional reality. Both Stephen King and E.L. Doctorow recommend that you create it step by step—incident by incident—to find your way to a first draft. This keeps the work spontaneous and real, while allowing your imagination to run at full throttle.

> "For first you write a sentence,
> And then you chop it small;
> Then mix the bits, and sort them out   Just as they chance to fall:
> The order of the phrases makes
> No difference at all."
>
> —Lewis Carroll

cc.   *Syntax* – the most effective order of words in a sentence; and sentences in a paragraph, etc.

dd. *Theme* – what the story's about: the Insanity of War, the Degradation of Poverty, the Transformative Effect of Love, the Intricate Complexity and Contradictions of Familial Ties, the Cathartic Effect of Art, etc. As clichéd as these might seem, you need a central idea to keep your intent in view. Even after completing many pages, or a draft, you might still not see it clearly; but eventually, by rewriting, cutting away the excess words, you will glimpse the idea you had hoped to deposit in the reader's imagination.

> "Writing comes more easily if you have something to say."
>
> — Sholem Asch

ee. *Voice* – who's telling the story—the speaker who pulls the reader into, and through, the narrative.

"You do not need to leave your room. Remain sitting at your table and listen. Do not even listen, simply wait, be quite still and solitary. The world will freely offer itself to you to be unmasked, it has no choice, it will roll in ecstasy at your feet."

—Franz Kafka

12. The Stillness of Reading

Writing is reading and reading is writing. You learn one from the other. There is a stillness in reading; and if we're engaged with what we read, our imaginations are stimulated, and our minds easily conjure up images from the words. You and the book are alone—even in a crowded room—your eyes locked onto the page, the words transposed into the sights, sounds, and smells hidden in your mind.

> "Reading offers a heady way of identifying with another, mirroring and reinforcing the self."
>
> —Mark Kingwell, *Beyond the Book*

While it is possible to learn something of dramatic and comedic story technique from watching visual media (TV, movies, etc.), reading remains the single most important resource we have to acquire the necessary tools for writing prose. Many writers echo Stephen King's statement: "If you want to be a writer, you must do two things above all others: read a lot and write a lot. There's no way around these two things that I'm aware of, no shortcut."

Reading stretches the imagination. It's where new sentence structure is assimilated; and where we acquire new words (even if,

> "He that reads and grows no wiser seldom suspects his own deficiency, but complains of hard words and obscure sentences, and asks why books are written which cannot be understood."
>
> —Samuel Johnson, *The Idler*

initially, we have no clue as to their exact meaning, we will intuit the sense of the word, and eventually learn its purpose). To a writer, indiscriminate reading is the equivalent of a college education.

> "Read, read, read. Read everything—trash, classics, good and bad, and see how they do it. Just like a carpenter who works as an apprentice and studies the master. Read! You'll absorb it. Then write. If it is good, you'll find out. If it's not, throw it out the window."
>
> —William Faulkner

John Holt, in his essay *How Teachers Make Children Hate Reading*, relates observing how his fifth graders, forced to analyse the books they read, began to hate reading. He decided to let them decide what they wanted to read, and even to discard a book if they found it boring. One girl, who had had difficulties rising to 'grade level', promptly started reading Dr. Seuss and other books of the same ilk. Holt then suggested she read *National Velvet*, which she did and enjoyed, although it was harder. A few months later, he was surprised to find her reading *Moby Dick*. He asked her if she found it heavy going. "Oh sure," she said, "but I just skip over those parts and go on to the next good part."

We cannot learn to write good prose by watching visual media. We might learn something about plot and pacing—or about writing for media—but we will not learn how to write *to be read*.

> "The best way to become a successful writer is to read good writing, remember it, and then forget where you remember it from."
>
> —Gene Fowler

There is a world of difference between reading and watching. Staring at a screen (movie, TV, computer or phone, or some other techno device) is seeing life through someone else's imagination. It is usually action fraught with noise and animation, all vying for your attention, storming your senses. Reading, conversely, happens in stillness—

all the noise and animation is created in your imagination *by you.*

This idea is reinforced by Jerzy Kosinski. (Interviewed many years ago, Kosinski refers to TV but we believe his theory applies to all forms of visual technology):

"Today, people are involved in the most common denominator, the *visual.* It requires no education to watch TV. It knows no age limit. Your child could watch the same program you do. Witness its role in the homes of the old and incurably sick. *Television is everywhere. It has the immediacy which the evocative medium of language doesn't. Language requires some inner triggering; television doesn't. [Italics ours]* The image is immediately accessible, i.e., extremely attractive. And, I think, ultimately deadly, because it turns the viewer into a bystander... Television is a very pleasing medium; one is always the observer. The life of discomfort is always accorded to others, and even this is disqualified, since one program immediately disqualifies the preceding one. *Literature does not have this ability to soothe. You have to evoke, and by evoking, you yourself have to provide your own inner setting. When you read about a man who dies, part of you dies with him because you have to recreate his dying inside your head." [Italics ours]—The Paris Review*

This 'evoking' puts you in charge. Sitting in the muddle of your own thoughts, you alone have full authority over all you create.

The following is a *partial* reading list—not definitive, personal only— (reading *is* intensely subjective), of some books that we've found liberating, memorable, or informative:

1.   *1984* – George Orwell. His final gasp, a chilling work based on elements of his—and our—world, projected into a futuristic novel

terrifyingly close to reality. It's possible that the story Orwell created now exists in reality in the Western world, and in certain totalitarian countries (e.g. North Korea).

2. *The Adventure of English* – Melwyn Bragg relates how the English language survived and flourished over centuries. Following the Norman invasion of 1066, the English that had evolved up to 1066 (a mix of Celtic, Anglo-Saxon, and Danish words) was in danger of being subsumed by the French. "... the Normans came with an alien tongue and they imposed it. On Christmas Day 1066, William was crowned in Westminster Abbey. The service was conducted in English and Latin. William spoke French throughout... French ruled. And the French language of rule, of power, of authority, of superiority, buried the English language." English, however, like some large, sloth-like, voracious animal, simply absorbed those French words it found useful, anglicised them, and added them to its own stock. "It has been estimated that in the three centuries following the Conquest perhaps as many as ten thousand French words colonized English..."

> "Books are my friends when nobody else can be; they offer a form of intimacy nothing else does. They do not make me a better person, but they give me respite from the incessant noise of existence."
>
> —Mark Kingwell, *Beyond the Book*

3. *Adventures in the Screen Trade* – William Goldman. Pertinent insight into the craft of writing screenplays. Offers an understanding of the inanity of the mainstream movie industry from the perspective of a successful screenwriter.

4. *Alice's Adventures in Wonderland* – Lewis Carroll. Mad and delirious, a vivid demonstration of how dreaming can morph into magical surrealism.

5. *Animal Farm* – George Orwell. A simple but enormously effective parable that allowed Orwell to spoof Stalin, and which clearly illustrates how "All animals are equal but some are more equal than others."

6. *Anna Karenina* – Leo Tolstoy. A love story that might prove instructive to teenage readers.

7. *Annals of the Former World* – John McPhee. Originally published in five volumes (in McPhee's simple but expressive prose), these six

hundred and sixty pages, a history of Earth viewed through geology—its extinctions, glacial dominances, continental collisions, and ocean emergences, all before man arrived—offers the reader the sensation of venturing, mouse-like, out into a dark, vast, rock-strewn, erupting plain.

8. *The Art of the Novel* – Milan Kundera. Ruminations on the form by one of the twentieth century's most astute writers.

> "The man who does not read good books has no advantage over the man who can't read them."
>
> —Mark Twain

9. *Autobiography* – Benvenuto Cellini. A not impartial, but highly engaging life of a successful artisan, set against the violence of the Renaissance.

10. *Blood and Daring* – John Boyko. A remarkably well-written history, illustrating how fear of US expansionism during the Civil War hastened Canadian Confederation—a turbulent and crucial four years viewed through the lives of six individuals.

11. *The Book of Laughter and Forgetting* – Milan Kundera achieved the same kind of authority in this 'novel' as Vonnegut does in *Slaughterhouse Five*. A central *voice* so strong that disparate secondary voices flow seamlessly from one to the next, supporting the predominant *theme*.

12. *Bouvard et Pécuchet* – Gustave Flaubert. Unfinished at the time of his death, this was to be the first of Flaubert's two books exposing middle class stupidity. The Penguin edition includes *The Dictionary of Received Ideas*. Succinct, painfully wry.

13. *Brideshead Revisited* – Evelyn Waugh. A sharp-etched look at the complexity of human relationships affected by having—and not having—religion and money. Waugh offers compassionate insight into the lives of people one might not normally care about.

14. *The Broken Estate* – James Wood. A surpassing and perceptive collection of essays on influential writers.

15. *The Call of the Wild* – Jack London. Having lived through, and almost died in, the Yukon Gold Rush, London conveys the excitement and the fear of man living within nature.

16. *Candide* – Voltaire – Life's great lessons in one hundred and forty-four pages of simple prose.

> "Before I start writing a novel I read Candide over again so that I may have in the back of my mind the touch-stone of that lucidity, grace and wit."
>
> —W. Somerset Maugham

17. *Catch-22* – Joseph Heller – Heller's view of the conflict between intelligent humans and the military during war might be even funnier, and more pertinent now, than when first published.

18. *The Catcher in the Rye* – J. D. Salinger. Set in 1950s America, the First Person voice of Holden Caulfield still snags the reader.

19. *Charlotte's Web* – E.B. White. A simple parable demonstrating compassion, and how easily one can misjudge passing events.

20. *The Collected Stories of John Cheever* – A master of the short story, Cheever's lifetime collection is a formidable demonstration of how to turn glimpses of human frailty into compelling tales.

21. *Confessions* – Jean Jacques Rousseau. Rousseau was much accused of fabrication (and self-absorption) in the telling, but his memoir immerses the reader in eighteenth-century France.

22. *David Copperfield* – Charles Dickens. This autobiographical novel is Dickens at the height of his ability, effortlessly bagging the reader with captivating incidents, looming characters, and surprising narrative.

23. *The Chrysalids* – John Wyndham. One of Wyndham's "logical fantasies," in print since 1955—the post-apocalyptic world he creates seems frighteningly possible.

24. *Day of the Locust* – Nathaniel West. A grim look at the underbelly of Hollywood in the 1930s. West's novel touchingly reveals the desolation of a society obsessed with modernity and celebrity, and consumed by hopelessness.

25. *Don Quixote* – Cervantes. The first modern novel. Still a contender for possibly the greatest.

26. *The Ecology of Commerce* – Paul Hawken. A simple, eloquent, and well-researched examination of the connection between corporations and the destruction of our natural world.

27. *The Elements of Style* – William Strunk Jr. and E.B. White. Brief, simple, and apparently timeless. As a primer on writing effective prose, there are few as explicit.

28. *Flaubert's Parrot* by Julian Barnes. Not so much a novel as a passionate examination of Gustave's eccentricity, intelligence, and work.

> "Any fool may write a valuable book by chance, if he will only tell us what he heard and saw with veracity."
> —Thomas Gray

29. *The General in his Labyrinth* – Gabriel García Márquez. A fictional account of the last two years in the life of Simón José Antonio de la Santísima Trinidad Bolívar y Palacios, the General known as 'the liberator' who chased the Spanish from South America. Exotic, fascinating, and moving.

30. *The Ginger Man* – J.P. Donleavy – a sad, bawdy, cringing novel about a man who, out of egotistical, 'romantic,' selfishness, forsakes those closest to him.

31. *The Good Soldier Švejk* – Jaroslav Hašek. One of the great, influential, comic novels of the twentieth century. With soldiers like *Švejk* it might be possible to end war.

32. *Good-Bye to All That* – Robert Graves. A simple, evocative memoir showing how the poet survived the trenches of the Great War.

33. *The Grapes of Wrath* – John Steinbeck. Written almost in a semi-documentary style, Steinbeck, having wandered among families displaced by drought and economic hardship, centres his novel around the Joads, a sharecropper family on the edge of extinction during the Great Depression.

34. *The Great Gatsby* – F. Scott Fitzgerald defined 1920s America in his early work, particularly in this novel of unrequited love, a timeless look at the effect of untold wealth.

35. *Gulliver's Travels* – Jonathan Swift. Few have had as sharply pointed a quill as Swift, or have been able to de-bone human stupidity quite as cleanly.

36. *The Horse's Mouth* – Joyce Cary. A witty and touching depiction of the artistic temperament (*setting* is magically seen through the eyes of the protagonist, 67-year-old painter Gully Jimson). Few books have as strong a First Person voice, or are as eloquent in showing how character can drive narrative on.

37. *The Horse That Leaps Through Clouds* – Eric Enno Tamm. An overland journey from Moscow to Peking made by a Russian spy in

1906, reconstructed by Tamm in 2006, offers us a view of modern China.

> "I am by trade a novelist. It is, I think, a harmless trade, though it is not everywhere considered a respectable one. Novelists put dirty language into the mouths of their characters, and they show these characters fornicating or going to the toilet. Moreover, it is not a *useful* trade, as is that of the carpenter or the pastry cook. The novelist passes the time for you between one useful action and another; he helps to fill the gaps that appear in the serious fabric of living. He is mere entertainer, a sort of clown. He mimes, he makes grotesque gestures, he is pathetic or comic or sometimes both, he sends words spinning through the air like coloured balls."
>
> —Anthony Burgess,
> *The Clockwork Connection*

38. *How Fiction Works* – James Wood. Wood muses over what makes good fiction; and his insightful prognostications, to those seeking to approach writing as more than a trade, offer much to consider.

39. *Huckleberry Finn* – Mark Twain. A great novel with an odd ending. Twain achieves the impossible, illustrating how experience will gradually modify or change prejudice.

40. *I Served the King of England* – Bohumil Hrabal. A humorously rapid transit through a central, twentieth-century European country, as viewed through the eyes of a waiter.

41. *The Idiot* – Fyodor Dostoyevsky's great novel (an early anti-hero?), surprisingly funny.

42. *If on a winter's night a traveller* – Italo Calvino pushes the boundaries of narrative and the reader's willing suspension of disbelief, inviting him or her to take a pro-active role in the process.

43. *Indignation* – Philip Roth. Eloquent, short, this novel, a view of '50s collegiate America, offers sombre thoughts on life's vagaries.

44. *Jane Eyre* – Charlotte Brontë. A vulnerable young woman survives a loveless upbringing, her successful emergence into the world entirely dependent on maintaining strength of character. One of the great Victorian novels.

45. *Jude the Obscure* – Thomas Hardy. Unrelenting in its depiction of a stonemason facing adversity while seeking love and a basic existence. Edifying and compelling.

46. *Lady Chatterley's Lover* – D.H. Lawrence's depiction of sex remains one the most explicit and compassionate, containing also a keen set of observations on the British class system of the 1920s.

47. *The Life of Samuel Johnson* – James Boswell. One of the great biographies.

48. *The Life and Death of Peter Sellers* – Roger Lewis. A great modern biography in the tradition of Boswell. By revealing Sellers with much telling detail (as did Boswell with Johnson), Lewis saddens us with the ultimately tragic story of this extraordinary performer.

49. *Little Women* – Louisa May Alcott. A demonstration of how people (women) can recover from tremendous blows.

50. *Lord of the Flies* – William Golding. Reveals how dominated by base instincts humans are.

51. *The Loved One* – It is remarkable that Evelyn Waugh's novel, published in 1948, satirizing middle-class attitudes to death, still carries a punch in today's-almost-impossible-to-satirize-America.

52. *Madame Bovary* – Flaubert spent five years writing this novel, reading it aloud to friends, and agonizing over it line by line. Bovary, as a work of art, is dense, complex, and yet immediately accessible to the reader. In his words, "Madame Bovary, c'est moi."

53. *The Man Who Was Thursday* – G.K. Chesterton's anarchist comic fantasy reads like a dream.

54. *A Member of the Wedding* – Carson McCullers. A simple, evocative tale of yearning of a young girl isolated from conflict.

55. *Metamorphosis and Other Stories* – Franz Kafka's work, meant by the author to be destroyed after his death, gives us a fragmented sense of the surrealistic early twentieth century.

56. *Myself With Others* – Carlos Fuentes. Engaging essays on writing and politics.

57. *Nostromo* – Joseph Conrad – a long, rambling, historical novel that gradually pulls you into the violent history of South America.

58. *Nothing to Declare* – Julian Barnes. Well-written, thoughtful essays by this English writer of his lifetime relationship to France. Nine of the seventeen essays reveal intriguing aspects of Flaubert's approach to the writing of *Madame Bovary*.

> "Never lend books, for no one ever returns them; the only books I have in my library are books that other folk have lent me."
>
> —Anatole France

> "I write differently from what I speak, I speak differently from what I think, I think differently from the way I ought to think, and so it all proceeds into deepest darkness."
>
> —Franz Kafka

59. *Of Human Bondage* – Somerset Maugham. Often accused of being a master of cliché, Maugham has a tight grip on narrative; and although *OHB* resembles a Victorian novel—the story of a club-footed young man determined to succeed, afflicted with unrequited love—in size, is twentieth century in its outlook.

60. *On Writing* – Stephen King. Engaging. King's ruminations on how to write forceful stories offer useful advice and encouragement.

61. *One Flew Over the Cuckoo's Nest* – Ken Kesey. The protagonist, Randall Patrick McMurphy, along with the oppressive setting and eccentric characters, captivates the reader; although the First Person voice of Chief Bromden is sometimes buried in summary exposition, clouding the narrative. When the story finds open sky, however, 'Cuckoo's Nest' soars.

> "The rise of an educated reading public was linked inextricably to the emergence of democratic liberalism in the Western World. The development of the novel as a literary form is likewise conjoined with the idea of open public discourse and rational-critical debate."
>
> —Mark Kingwell, *Beyond the Book*

62. *One Hundred Years of Solitude* – Gabriel García Márquez's stunning achievement is *narrative* writ large—possibly the most successful of the magic-realist novels. Along with *characterization, theme,* sparse and telling detail, and minimal but quintessential *dialogue,* this work is a succinct example of what the novel form can achieve.

63. *The Ordeal of Gilbert Pinfold* – Evelyn Waugh's semi-comic and well-executed story is of an English novelist—himself?—on a cruise in the midst of a mental breakdown brought on by the overuse of pharmaceuticals.

64. *Promise at Dawn* – Romain Gary. An autobiographical tribute to his mother and her indomitable spirit by the accomplished French author.

65. *The Quiet American* – Graham Greene. Greene's moralistic tale, placed during the French occupation of Vietnam in the early '50s, written in simple prose, illustrates, compels, and touches.

66. *The Rabbit Novels* – in this tetralogy, John Updike examined eternal man, in twentieth-century America, and found frailty—a flawed antihero, modern in wants, ancient in needs.

67. *Ragtime* – E.L. Doctorow. An example of the novel ably revealing the time in which it's set (the turbulence of Edwardian America), combining fictional characters and historical figures.

68. *A Reader's Manifesto* – B. R. Myers. Myers surgically explores contemporary literature, finding much of it to rely on artifice and affectation.

> "The difference between journalism and literature is that journalism is unreadable and literature is not read."
>
> —Oscar Wilde

69. *Reuben, Reuben* – Peter De Vries. A trilogy in one novel. Three acutely-drawn characters in a narrative that (from the song of the title) proposes: "What a grand world this would be. If the men were all transported far beyond the northern sea."

70. *Roget's Thesaurus* – Peter Mark Roget. Metaphorically, it's the source of the Nile. You cannot hold all the words of the English language in your head, so why try?

71. *Satires* – Lewis Lapham. One of America's most gifted essayists, a writer who has consistently revealed the absurdity and naughtiness of the American oligarchy. Now publisher of *Lapham's Quarterly.*

72. Screenplays – For the screenwriter seeking methodology or just hoping to spark their thinking on screenwriting, any of the screenplays of great films will provide useful inspiration (e.g. CITIZEN KANE, LA DOLCE VITA, THE 400 BLOWS, THE THIRD MAN [originally a novella-length outline], NIGHT OF THE HUNTER, or any of the post-war Italian neo-realist films. Viewing movies is also useful (particularly those of the early '70s, e.g. FIVE EASY PIECES, SHAMPOO, CHINATOWN, THE KING OF MARVIN GARDENS, etc.).

73. *The Screenwriter Looks at the Screenwriter* – William Froug. The original edition (1972) contained interviews with Stirling Silliphant, Ernest Lehman and other screenwriters from the 1950s and '60s. Worth reading for the aspiring screenwriter, if it can be found.

74. *Slaughterhouse Five* – Kurt Vonnegut. No one writes like Vonnegut. At first glance, the prose appears to ramble, but there are no wasted

words, and he is adept at pulling the reader through his narrative at a furious clip.

75.   *Song of Ascent* – Gabriella Goliger. A collection of imaginative short stories centred on a Jewish family in Montreal.

76.   *Sons and Lovers* – strong in *setting, character* and *voice,* D. H. Lawrence on the eternal triangle—mother, son, son's lover.

77.   *The Sun Also Rises* – Ernest Hemingway. Though the central character reads as emotionally vague, Hemingway's realistic *dialogue* and sparse exposition places the reader right inside 1920s Paris and Spain.

78.   *The Third Policeman* – Flann O'Brien. Not published during the author's lifetime, this surreal Irish novel amuses and terrifies, illustrating the power of an over-wrought imagination (an Irish one) with an existential bent: "Is it about a bicycle?"

79.   *Three Men in a Boat* – Jerome K. Jerome. A classic Edwardian book of manly British humour.

80.   *Timebends* – Arthur Miller's autobiography. A thoughtful and fascinating self-examination of a life in the theatre and movies by one of America's most accomplished writers.

> "Art has always been the revenge of the human spirit upon the short-sighted."
>
> —Arthur Miller

81.   *The Tin Drum* – Günter Grass. As a large metaphor for Germany and the German people in the first half of the twentieth century, it's hard to trump Grass's first novel. His use of First and Third Person is an example of knowing how to break the rules.

82.   *Through the Safety Net* – Charles Baxter. Early Baxter, a story collection acutely observing the human condition at close range.

83.   *Too Loud a Solitude* – Bohumil Hrabal. A short, compelling, stream-of-consciousness novel, contemplating human existence, from inside the mind of a man operating a garbage incinerator to burn previously-imposed political culture (Nazi literature followed by that of Soviet Socialism).

84.   *True Grit* – Charles Portis. A potent example of strong voice and sparse but telling exposition.

85.   *Ulysses* – James Joyce – a year's read at least, containing enough rich prose, thought, and style to establish an academy, from the

writer many consider the twentieth century's pre-eminent literary explorer.

86. *United States, Essays 1952-1992* – Containing the bulk of Gore Vidal's essays. Vidal, a master of expository prose and one of our most astute critics, wrote eloquently on literature, history, and American politics.

> "History is the recital of facts represented as true. Fable, on the other hand, is the recital of facts represented as fiction."
>
> —Voltaire

87. *Vanity Fair* – William Makepeace Thackeray. The ultimately disillusioning story of Becky and Amelia contains all the elements of prose; one of the great Victorian novels.

88. *Ways of Escape* – Graham Greene. Greene's autobiographical history of how his stories came to be written offers personal observations on the novel.

89. *When the Shooting Stops... the Cutting Begins* – Ralph Rosenblum gives us an explicit description of the editing process in film, with lessons that apply exactly to writing.

90. *Wide Sargasso Sea* – Jean Rhys. Rhys turns *Jane Eyre* inside out, telling us the story of Mrs. Rochester, born on a warm, vibrant Caribbean island, ending in a room in a chilly English manor house, the one from which Jane hears a "distinct, formal, mirthless" laugh.

91. *Wind in the Willows* – any book with characters named Ratty, Mole, Badger, and Toad whets our wistful natures immediately.

> "Why is it that an inventor can sit in a room for five years with a sheet of paper and a pencil, and when he finally comes up with something, it's capital gain; but when writers do the same thing, it's current income, which is heavily taxed?"
>
> —Adam Smith

92. *Wise Blood* – Flannery O'Connor. A stringent, compassionate view of being Southern and poor in the United States. O'Connor was a zealous author, brooking no interference from her publisher over matters of subject or style.

93. *Winnie the Pooh, The House at Pooh Corner* – A.E. Milne. Yes, it did make Dorothy Parker "thwow up" but for the rest of us, the charm of Milne's characters is one of the true wonders of the early twentieth century. Too bad about the Disney connection.

94. *Wolf Hall* – Hilary Mantel – the first of a trilogy—a thick, comprehensive, but sparsely written story of how Thomas Cromwell became

Henry VIII's chief adviser and facilitator. Extremely well crafted and conceived, as is the second volume, *Bring on the Dead Bodies*.

95.   *Women in Love* – D. H. Lawrence's take on the complications, the hopelessness, and tenderness, of relationships between men and women.

96.   *The Writer's Chapbook* [Ed. George Plimpton]. A selection of intriguing and informative quotes by well-known writers on all aspects of writing; culled from the vast collection of interviews conducted by *The Paris Review* since the early 1950s.

97.   *Wuthering Heights* – Emily Brontë. Complex, violent, the story of Heathcliff's revenge on, and unrequited love for, Catherine enthrals and instructs.

98.   *The Year of Magical Thinking* – Joan Didion. With a remarkable absence of sentiment, Didion examines her grief at the sudden death of her husband and the abrupt hospitalization of her daughter.

Recommended short prose

These compelling and engaging stories and essays are a small selection of effective prose pieces.

From *Best American Short Stories of the Century*

My Dead Brother Comes to America	Alexander Godin
Defender of the Faith	Phillip Roth
Criers and Kibitzers, Kibitzers and Criers	Stanley Elkin
The Things They Carried	Tim O'Brien
You're Ugly Too	Lorrie Moore

From *Best American Short Stories 1987*

Private Debt / Public Holdings	Kent Haruf
The Other Miller	Tobias Wolff
The Interpretation of Dreams by Sigmund Freud: A Story	Daniel Stern
Milk	Ron Carlson

From the *MacMillan Anthology of American Literature Vol. II 3rd Edition*

Babylon Revisited	F. Scott Fitzgerald
The Short Happy Life of Francis Macomber	Ernest Hemingway
Barn Burning	William Faulkner

From *The Art of the Tale*

The Bound Man	Ilse Aichinger
The Child Screams and Looks	Russell Banks
Back at You First Love	Samuel Beckett
Action Will Be Taken	Heinrich Böll
A Distant Episode	Paul Bowles
The Adventure of a Traveller	Italo Calvino
The Adulterous Woman	Albert Camus
I Look Out For Ed Wolfe	Stanley Elkin
Communist	Richard Ford
The Conjurer Made Off With the Dish	Naguib Mahfouz
The Last Mohican	Bernard Malamud
Jewellery	Alberto Moravia
Doctor Safi	Mohammed Mrabet
XXII	Nathalie Sarraute
Death and the Maiden	Michel Tournier

From *Best European Fiction 2010*

Bulbjerg	Naja Marie Aidt
Ants and Bumblebees	Inga Ābele
Resistance	Stephan Enter

From *Best European Fiction 2011*

The Heart Fails Without Warning	Hilary Mantel
The Prophecy	Drago Jančar
The Evil Eye	Andrei Gelasimov
Hotel By a Railroad	Frode Grytten
Auntie Frosea	Iulian Ciocan
Dust	Stefan Sprenger
Trespasses	Éilís Ní Dhuibhne
Doctor Sot	Kevin Barry
Holes in People	Kristín Eiríksdóttir
Sex for Fridge	Zurab Lezhava

American Diary	Eric Laurrent
My Girlfriend	Mima Simić
Varneesh	Goran Samardžić

From *The Penguin Book of Canadian Short Stories*

The Lonely Goatherd	Lisa Moore
Dead Girls	Nancy Lee
Ray	Guy Vanderhaeghe

Non-Fiction from the *Norton Shorter Reader 6th Edition*

Chicago August 24-29,[1968]	Norman Mailer
What Writers Do	John Gardner
Denmark and the Jews	Hannah Arendt
The Boy Scout Handbook	Paul Fussell
A Passion to Learn	Paul West

Acknowledgements

The authors gratefully acknowledge the permissions granted to reproduce the copyrighted material in this book.

Permission-gathering is complicated, imprecise, and time consuming. To quote from the work of others, authors, under copyright law, are obliged to obtain permission, usually at the cost of a license fee to the copyright holder—the quotes, in most books, being few and the licence fees light.

For this work, we wanted to offer the reader the wisdom of those (as many as possible) who had excelled at prose-writing. With over 150 quotes not in the public domain, however, paying a fee for each (at $50-75 per) would have prohibited EP's publication. Yet we were determined to publish the book as we had imagined it, and understood that we would need to solicit the generous participation of all.

Early on, we obtained the consent of a number of authors, publishers, and literary agents who applauded our intent and granted us permission. With many of those we approached, however, our emails and snail-mails went unanswered for months; or our replies to their responses were disregarded; or the copyright holder simply did not respond. Many who were contacted were adamant about charging fees. This seemed an insurmountable hurdle, for paying a fee to some and not to others *when all were given to understand that no license fees would be paid to any* ("favoured nations") would have been fraudulent.

We considered paraphrasing the quotes; but, in a work illustrating arresting prose, that seemed absurd. This left us with 'fair use', the publishing term for that courtesy extended by the copyright holder to allow an author to quote a limited number of words *without* permission if used for purposes of "criticism, comment, news reporting, teaching, scholarship or research" (Section 107, 1976 Copyright Act).

We found little agreement in the industry as to the number of words considered 'fair use.' Some of the agents and publishers we approached avoided the question unless prodded (and sometimes not responding even then). One agent told us 200 words; *The Idiot's Guide to Publishing* suggested 250, as was reluctantly allowed by the permissions manager at a venerable publishing house. *The New York Public Library – Writer's Guide to Style and Usage* (HarperCollins 1994) put the norm at 300 to 500 words; and somewhere on the internet we saw 400 (for America only).

Finally, on Pearson PLC's website we found: "No more than 500 words from any one source may be quoted in a work (text or supplement) without permission." Pearson, as the world's largest book publisher (in partnership with Bertelsmann combining the forces of Random House and all its imprints and those of the Penguin Group and all their imprints) had, it seemed to us, set a serviceable benchmark—a limit that would allow accurate expression of the author's thought without infringing *on the intent* of their copyright.

Much effort was spent to contact the copyright owners of the material included herein, and in instances where this has not proved possible, or for any errors, we offer our apologies.

'Creative Writing 101' from *Bagombo Snuff Box: Uncollected Short Fiction* by Kurt Vonnegut, copyright © 1999 by Kurt Vonnegut. Reprinted by permission of G.P. Putnam's Sons, a division of Penguin Group (USA) LLC.

Figures of Speech (*Harper's* editorial) by Lewis Lapham. Reprinted by permission of the author.

The General in His Labyrinth by Gabriel Garcia Marquez. Copyright © Gabriel Garcia Marquez. Published originally by Alfred A. Knopf Inc. Reprinted by permission of Penguin Random House.

The Ghost Writer by Philip Roth. Excerpt from "Maestro." Copyright © 1979 by Philip Roth. Reprinted by permission of Farrar, Straus and Giroux, LLC.

The Habit of Being: Letters of Flannery O'Connor [Ed. Sally Fitzgerald]. Except from "Part I: Up North and Getting Home, 1948-1952." Copyright © 1979 by Regina O'Connor. Reprinted by permission of Farrar, Straus & Giroux, LLC.

The Handyman by Penelope Mortimer. Copyright © Penelope Mortimer, 1983. Reprinted by permission of Sheil Land Associates Ltd.

The Horse's Mouth by Joyce Cary. Copyright © Joyce Cary 1944. Originally published by Michael Joseph. Reprinted by permission of the Joyce Cary Estate and the Andrew Lownie Literary Agency Ltd.

How Fiction Works by James Wood. Excerpts from "Language" and "Truth, Convention, Realism". Copyright © by James Wood. Reprinted by permission of Farrar, Straus and Giroux, LLC.

How Teachers Make Children Hate Reading by John Holt. Reprinted by permission of Sentient Publications.

Jack London, Hemingway and the Constitution by E.L Doctorow. Copyright © E.L. Doctorow. Originally published by Random House, 1993. Reprinted by permission of Penguin Random House.

Maedele from *Song of Ascent* by Gabriella Golinger. Reprinted by permission of the author. Originally published by Raincoast, 2000.

Myself With Others by Carlos Fuentes. Excerpt from "Cervantes, or The Critique of Reading." Copyright © 1988 by Carlos Fuentes. Published by Farrar, Straus and Giroux, 1990.

Ninety-Nine Novels: The Best in English since 1939 — A Personal Choice by Anthony Burgess Copyright © Anthony Burgess 1984, Summit Books. Reprinted by permission of the David Higham Agency.

Palimpsest by Gore Vidal. Copyright © Gore Vidal. Originally published by Penguin, 1996. Reprinted by permission of Penguin Random House.

Parade's End by Ford Maddox Ford. Copyright © Ford Maddox Ford. Carcanet Press. Reprinted by permission of the David Higham Agency.

The Paris Review. Excerpted from an interview with Hortense Calisher. Copyright © 1987, 2014 by *The Paris Review*. Reprinted with permission by The Wylie Agency, LLC. All Rights Reserved.

The Paris Review. Excerpted from an interview with Philip Roth. Copyright © 1984, 2014 by *The Paris Review*. Reprinted with permission by The Wylie Agency, LLC. All Rights Reserved.

The Paris Review. Excerpted from an interview with William Kennedy. Copyright © 1989, 2014 by *The Paris Review*. Reprinted with permission by The Wylie Agency, LLC. All Rights Reserved.

The Reader's Manifesto by B.R. Myers. Reprinted by permission of Melville House Publishing.

Stained Glass from *Through the Safety Net* by Charles Baxter. Reprinted by permission of the author. Originally published by Vintage, 1998.

The Third Man by Graham Greene, copyright © Graham Greene. Originally published by The Viking Press, 1950. Reprinted by permission of the David Higham Agency.

The Tin Drum by Günter Grass and Breon Mitchell. Copyright © 1959 by Hermann Luchterhand Verlag GmbH. Translation copyright © by Breon Mitchell. Reprinted with permission by Houghton Mifflin Harcourt Publishing Company. All Rights Reserved.

Too Loud a Solitude by Bohumil Hrabal. Copyright © 1976 Bohumil Hrabal. English translation copyright © 1990 by Harcourt, Inc. Reprinted by permission of the Houghton Mifflin Harcourt Publishing Company. All Rights Reserved.

United States, Essays 1952-1992 by Gore Vidal. Copyright © 1993 by Gore Vidal. Reprinted by permission by Penguin Random House.

Ways of Escape by Graham Greene, copyright © Graham Greene. Originally published by The Bodley Head 1980. Reprinted by permission of the David Higham Agency.

Why I Write by Joan Didion, copyright © 1976 Joan Didion. Originally published in *The New York Times Book Review*. Reprinted by permission of the author.

References

The Adventure of English by Melwyn Bragg. Published by Arcade Publishing, 2011.

Advice to Writers by Jon Winokur. Published by Vintage, 2000.

The Art of the Novel by Milan Kundera. Published by Grove Press, 1988.

The Brothers Goncourt Diaries by Jules & Edmond de Goncourt. Published by *Catch-22* by Joseph Heller. Published by Scribner, 1961.

The Collected Stories by John McGahern. Published by Faber & Faber, 1992.

Creationists by E.L. Doctorow. Published by Random House, 2007.

Dennis Potter, A Biography by Humphrey Carpenter. Published by Faber & Faber, 1998.

Essays of George Orwell, Politics and the English Language. Published by Horizon, 1946.

Evelyn Waugh: The Later Years 1939-1960. Published in America by W.W. Norton & Company, 1992.

The Ginger Man by J.P. Donleavy. Published by Corgi Books, 1963.

The Good Soldier Švejk by Jaroslav Hašek. Published by A. Synek Publishers, 1923.

Lady Chatterley's Lover by D.H. Lawrence. Published by Mandrake Press, 1928.

Music by Night by Aldous Huxley. Published by Chatto & Windus, 1931.

The New York Public Library - Writer's Guide to Style and Usage [Ed. Andrea J. Sutcliffe]. Published by HarperCollins, 1994.

Nine Stories by J.D. Salinger. Published by Little Brown, 1953.

Nineteen Eighty-Four by George Orwell. Published by Secker & Warburg, 1949.

The Norton Reader, Sixth Edition Shorter [Arthur M. Eastman, General Editor] W.W. Norton 1984. (*The Eureka Phenomenon*, Isaac Asimov / *Education By Poetry*, Robert Frost)

On Writing, A Memoir of the Craft by Stephen King. Published by Simon & Schuster, 2000.

Oral Pleasures by Jerzy Kosinski. Published by Grove Atlantic, 2012

The Outsider by Albert Camus. Published by Éditions Gallimard, 1942

The Oxford Companion to the Mind [Ed. Richard L. Gregory]. Published by Oxford University Press 1987.

The Portable Graham Greene [Ed. Philip Stratford]. Published by Viking Press, 1973.

Reporting the Universe by E.L. Doctorow, Published by Harvard University Press, 2009.

Reuben, Reuben by Peter De Vries. Published by Little Brown, 1964. (Republished 2014 by the University of Chicago Press).

The Sense of an Ending by Frank Kermode. Published by Oxford University Press, 1967.

Song of Ascent by Gabriella Goliger. Published by Raincoast Books 2000.

The Third Policeman by Flann O'Brian. Published by MacGibbon & Kee, 1967.

The Wapshot Chronicle by John Cheever. Published by Harper & Row, 1957.

"Posterity is just around the corner."
—George S. Kaufman

MORE FROM BARAKA BOOKS